✧ *Companions for the Journey* ✧

Praying with Dante

✦ *Companions for the Journey* ✦

Praying with Dante

by
James J. Collins

Saint Mary's Press
Christian Brothers Publications
Winona, Minnesota

Genuine recycled paper with 10% post-consumer waste.
Printed with soy-based ink.

The publishing team for this book included Michael Wilt, development editor; Cheryl Drivdahl, copy editor; James H. Gurley, production editor and typesetter; Cären Yang, cover designer; Sam Thiewes, illustrator; produced by the graphics division of Saint Mary's Press.

The acknowledgments continue on page 116.

Printed in the United States of America

Printing: 9 8 7 6 5 4 3 2 1

Year: 2008 07 06 05 04 03 02 01 00

ISBN 0-88489-674-9

Library of Congress Cataloging-in-Publication Data

Collins, James J., 1938–
    Praying with Dante / by James J. Collins.
    p. cm. — (Companions for the journey)
Includes bibliographical references.
ISBN 0-88489-674-9 (pbk. : alk. paper)
    1. Meditations. 2. Dante Alighieri, 1265–1321—Religion. 3. Catholic Church—Prayer-books and devotions—English. I. Title. II. Series.
BX2182.2 C64 2000
242'.802—dc21

                                             00-008145

✧ Contents ✧

✧ Series Foreword ✧

Companions for the Journey

Just as food is required for human life, so are companions. Indeed, the word *companions* comes from two Latin words: *com*, meaning "with," and *panis*, meaning "bread." Companions nourish our heart, mind, soul, and body. They are also the people with whom we can celebrate the sharing of bread.

Perhaps the most touching stories in the Bible are about companionship: the Last Supper, the wedding feast at Cana, the sharing of the loaves and the fishes, and Jesus' breaking of bread with the disciples on the road to Emmaus. Each incident of companionship with Jesus revealed more about his mercy, love, wisdom, suffering, and hope. When Jesus went to pray in the Garden of Olives, he craved the companionship of the Apostles. They let him down. But God sent the Spirit to inflame the hearts of the Apostles, and they became faithful companions to Jesus and to one another.

Throughout history, other faithful companions have followed Jesus and the Apostles. These saints and mystics have also taken the journey from conversion, through suffering, to resurrection. Just as they were inspired by the holy people who went before them, so too may you be inspired by these saints and mystics and take them as your companions on your spiritual journey.

The Companions for the Journey series is a response to the spiritual hunger of Christians. This series makes available the rich spiritual teachings of mystics and guides whose wisdom can help us on our pilgrimage. As you complete the last meditation in each volume, it is hoped that you will feel supported, challenged, and affirmed by a soul-companion on your spiritual journey.

The spiritual hunger that has emerged over the last twenty years is a great sign of renewal in Christian life. People fill retreat programs and workshops on topics in spirituality. The demand for spiritual directors exceeds the number available. Interest in the lives and writings of saints and mystics is increasing as people search for models of whole and holy Christian life.

Praying with Dante

Praying with Dante is more than just a book about the spirituality of Dante Alighieri, the great Italian poet. This book seeks to engage you in praying in the way that Dante did about issues and themes that were central to his experience. Each meditation can enlighten your understanding of his spirituality and lead you to reflect on your own experience.

The goal of *Praying with Dante* is that you will discover Dante's rich spirituality and integrate his spirit and wisdom into your relationship with God, with your brothers and sisters, and with your own heart and mind.

Suggestions for Praying with Dante

Meet Dante, a fascinating companion for your pilgrimage, by reading the introduction to this book. It provides a brief biography of Dante and an outline of the major themes of his spirituality.

Once you meet Dante, you will be ready to pray with him and to encounter God, your sisters and brothers, and yourself in new and wonderful ways. To help your prayer, here are some suggestions that have been part of the tradition of Christian spirituality:

Create a sacred space. Jesus said, "Whenever you pray, go into your room and shut the door and pray to your [God] who is in secret; and your [God] who sees in secret will reward you" (Matthew 6:6). Solitary prayer is best done in a place where you can have privacy and silence, both of which can be luxuries in the life of busy people. If privacy and silence are not possible, create a quiet, safe place within yourself, perhaps while riding to and from work, while sitting in line at the dentist's office, or while waiting for someone. Do the best you can, knowing that a loving God is present everywhere. Whether the meditations in this book are used for solitary prayer or with a group, try to create a prayerful mood with candles, meditative music, an open Bible, or a crucifix.

Open yourself to the power of prayer. Every human experience has a religious dimension. All of life is suffused with God's presence. So remind yourself that God is present as you begin your period of prayer. Do not worry about distractions. If something keeps intruding during your prayer, spend some time talking with God about it. Be flexible because God's spirit blows where it will.

Prayer can open your mind and widen your vision. Be open to new ways of seeing God, people, and yourself. As you open yourself to the spirit of God, different emotions are evoked, such as sadness from tender memories, or joy from a celebration recalled. Our emotions are messages from God that can tell us much about our spiritual quest. Also, prayer strengthens our will to act. Through prayer, God can touch our will and empower us to live according to what we know is true.

Finally, many of the meditations in this book will call you to employ your memories, your imagination, and the circumstances of your life as subjects for prayer. The great mystics and saints realized that they had to use all their resources to know God better. Indeed, God speaks to us continually and touches us constantly. We must learn to listen and feel with all the means that God has given us.

Come to prayer with an open mind, heart, and will.

Preview each meditation before beginning. After you have placed yourself in God's presence, spend a few moments previewing the readings and especially the reflection activities. Several reflection activities are given in each meditation because different styles of prayer appeal to different personalities or personal needs. **Note that each meditation has more reflection activities than can be done during one prayer**

period. Therefore, select only one or two reflection activities each time you use a meditation. Do not feel compelled to complete all the reflection activities.

Read meditatively. Each meditation offers you a story about Dante and one or more readings from his writings. Take your time reading. If a particular phrase touches you, stay with it. Relish its feelings, meanings, and concerns.

Use the reflections. Following the readings is a short reflection in commentary form, which is meant to give perspective to the readings. Then you are offered several ways of meditating on the readings and the theme of the prayer. You may be familiar with the different methods of meditating, but in case you are not, they are described briefly here:

✦ *Repeated short prayer or mantra:* One means of focusing your prayer is to use a *mantra,* or "prayer word." The mantra may be a single word or a short phrase taken from the readings or the Scriptures. For example, a short prayer for meditation 2 in this book might simply be "God, fill me with wonder." Repeated slowly in harmony with your breathing, the mantra helps you center your heart and mind on one action or attribute of God.

✦ *Lectio divina:* This type of meditation is "divine studying," a concentrated reflection on the word of God or the wisdom of a spiritual writer. Most often in *lectio divina,* you will be invited to read a passage several times and then concentrate on one or two sentences, pondering their meaning for you and their effect on you. *Lectio divina* commonly ends with formulation of a resolution.

✦ *Guided meditation:* In this type of meditation, our imagination helps us consider alternative actions and likely consequences. Our imagination helps us experience new ways of seeing God, our neighbors, ourselves, and nature. When Jesus told his followers parables and stories, he engaged their imagination. In this book, you are invited to follow several guided meditations.

One way of doing a guided meditation is to read the scene or story several times, until you know the outline and can recall it when you enter into reflection. Or before your prayer time, you may wish to record the meditation on a tape recorder. If so, remember to allow pauses for reflection between phrases and to speak with a slow, peaceful pace and tone. Then, during prayer, when you have finished the readings and the reflection commentary, you can turn on your recording of the meditation and be led through it. If you find your own voice too distracting, ask a friend to make the tape for you.

✦ *Examen of consciousness:* The reflections often will ask you to examine how God has been speaking to you in your past and present experience—in other words, the reflections will ask you to examine your awareness of God's presence in your life.

✦ *Journal writing:* Writing is a process of discovery. If you write for any length of time, stating honestly what is on your mind and in your heart, you will unearth much about who you are, how you stand with your God, what deep longings reside in your soul, and more. For some reflections, you may wish to write a dialogue with Jesus or someone else. If you have never used writing as a means of meditation, try it. Reserve a special notebook for your journal writing. If desired, you can go back to your entries at a future time for an examen of consciousness.

✦ *Action:* Occasionally, a reflection will suggest singing a favorite hymn, going out for a walk, or undertaking some other physical activity. Actions can be meaningful forms of prayer.

Using the Meditations for Group Prayer

If you wish to use the meditations for community prayer, these suggestions may help:

✦ Read the theme to the group. Call the community into the presence of God, using the short opening prayer. Invite one or two participants to read one or both readings on Dante. If you use both readings, observe the pause between them.

✦ The reflection commentary may be used as a reading, or it may be omitted, depending on the needs and interests of the group.

✦ Select one of the reflection activities for your group. Allow sufficient time for your group to reflect, to recite a centering prayer or mantra, to accomplish a studying prayer (*lectio divina*), or to finish an examen of consciousness. Depending on the group and the amount of available time, you may want to invite the participants to share their reflections, responses, or petitions with the group.

✦ Reading the words from the Scriptures may serve as a summary of the meditation.

✦ If a formulated prayer or a psalm is given as a closing, it may be recited by the entire group. Or you may ask participants to offer their own prayers for the closing.

Now you are ready to begin praying with Dante, a faithful and caring companion on this stage of your spiritual journey. It is hoped that you will find him to be a true soul-companion.

✧ Preface ✧

Most people today do not find Dante's works very "reader-friendly." His writings are difficult and complex, even for those who are well educated. Dante was a formidable intellectual: a scholar of vast learning, an original philosopher, and the only significant "lay theologian" of the Middle Ages. He often held views quite different from those of the great authorities in philosophy and theology—Plato, Aristotle, Saint Augustine of Hippo, and Saint Thomas Aquinas—although he was deeply indebted to all of them. He was also profoundly influenced by the mystical writings of Saint Bernard and Saint Bonaventure, and possibly the works of Saint Hildegard of Bingen, Mechtild of Magdeburg, and other medieval mystics. He was inspired by the lives of Saint Francis of Assisi and Saint Clare of Assisi. A great "cloud of witnesses" enriched and guided his life, thoughts, and writings.

After many years of studying philosophy, theology, and mysticism, Dante wanted to share the human and divine wisdom he had discovered with those who were unfortunately, for various reasons, prevented from learning Latin (the language of medieval books and lectures) or from attending schools and universities. So he decided to write his major works in the language of the people, the common Italian. This was a bold innovation, severely criticized and ridiculed by professional scholars. He anticipated their objections by writing a treatise in Latin, *The Eloquence of the Vernacular (De Vulgari Eloquentia)*, justifying the use of the common language for lofty themes.

Before he wrote his most enduring masterpiece, *The Comedy (La Commedia)*, he began, but never finished, a work intended to be an encyclopedic feast of knowledge: *The Banquet*

(Il Convivio). In his opening words Dante humbly admitted that he merely sat at the feet of those seated at the blessed table of wisdom. Those few feasted on the "Bread of angels"; he simply gathered the crumbs they let fall. But he experienced such sweetness from what he received, that out of compassion he wanted to share with those wandering around "feeding on grass and acorns" his rich bounty. He considered himself a friend of every human being and was saddened by any deficiency or deprivation suffered by anyone he loved.

Dante realized that most people, because of "the pressures of family and civic responsibilities," are prevented from feasting on wisdom, although they have an aching hunger for it. So, out of love and compassion, he offered all his fellow humans— "women, no less than men"—his *Banquet* as bread for their journey of life. Dante is thus a true "companion": one who shares his bread (*pane* in Italian) with (*con* in Italian) us all.

In this "companion book" I joyfully present for reflection passages from *The Banquet*, *The New Life (La Vita Nuova)*, *The Comedy*, and other works and letters by Dante. In those three named major works, Dante often developed the theme of life as a journey or pilgrimage to God, whose love, wisdom, and power are the "Bread of angels," which sustains us now and will completely satisfy all our hungers and desires in a heavenly banquet.

The English translations from Dante's works in this book are my own, based on the Italian and Latin critical text of the 1984 edition of the *Enciclopedia Dantesca*, volume 6, edited by Umberto Bosco. All cites for Dante's works refer to that text. I am deeply indebted to the masterly English translations of *The Divine Comedy* by Charles Singleton and by Mark Musa. I depended as well on Christopher Ryan's English translation of *The Banquet* and Mark Musa's translation of *The New Life*. In addition I used Donald Nicholl's translations of Dante's works in *Monarchy, and Three Political Letters* as a basis for my own translations. I also consulted the biographies of Dante by Giovanni Boccaccio *(Vita di Dante)* and by Leonardo Bruni *(Life of Dante)*, in English translations edited by Charles Dinsmore, as well as Boccaccio's biography in the original Italian *(Trattatello in Laude di Dante)*, edited by Pier Giorgio Ricci.

In citing Dante's works I have departed from the traditional use of roman numerals and have instead used arabic numerals. Excerpts from *The Comedy* are sometimes given in Dante's tercet form, but longer citations are presented in standard prose style. Cites to *The Comedy* are given with the name of the part (*Inferno, Purgatory,* or *Paradise*), followed by the canto number and then the verse number or numbers—for example, *Inferno* 3:12–15. Cites to *The Banquet* are given by book number, chapter, and verse or verses—*Banquet* 1,3:3–5. Cites to *The Monarchy (De Monarchia)* and *The Eloquence of the Vernacular* are by chapter and verse—*Monarchy* 3:15; *Eloquence* 1:4–5. *The New Life* is a series of sonnets followed by Dante's comments, numbered sequentially; I have rendered them in plain prose and referenced them by their sequential number—*New Life* 1. Cites to *The Letter to Can Grande* are by numbered paragraph—*Letter to Can Grande* 12. Cites to Dante's *Epistles* are by numbered paragraph—*Epistle XII* 9.

Grateful acknowledgment should be given to Joseph Stoutzenberger, one of the first authors in this series of companion books (coauthor of *Praying with Francis of Assisi,* 1989), who suggested that I write this book. I am also profoundly grateful to my typist, Jacqueline DeLeo, whose excellent work and spiritual support helped to make this book a reality.

✧ Introduction ✧

A Biography of Dante

Compiling a detailed biography of Dante is quite impossible because we know relatively few facts about his life. His first biographer, fellow Florentine Giovanni Boccaccio (1313–1375), who knew personally the people and circumstances of Dante's life, wrote the highly romanticized *Life of Dante*, colored by his great admiration for Dante. Though the basic information is reliable, he embellished his story with many anecdotes and legendary elements. A more sober and scientific account was written later by Leonardo Bruni (1369–1444) to correct the somewhat gossipy and laudatory nature of Boccaccio's narrative. Many biographies of Dante have been written over the centuries, but his personality, spiritual life, and many aspects of his public life remain mysterious and elusive. To what extent he reveals his soul in his writings remains a matter of scholarly debate. Yet his intellectual achievements, his prophetic mission for peace and justice, his defeats and triumphs, and especially his journey to hell, purgatory, and paradise—culminating in a face-to-face vision of God—continue to fascinate readers and scholars to this day.

Dante's Childhood

Dante was born in 1265 and baptized at Easter in his "beautiful Saint John," a splendid baptistery that still stands in the center of old Florence. Little is known of his parents and childhood, although life in Florence in the late thirteenth century is well documented. Dante's family could be described as upwardly mobile middle class with outstanding debts. Even though his father was descended from noble blood and had inherited some properties, the Alighieris were not among the powerful aristocratic families that ruled Florence. Dante's mother, Bella, died when Dante was only five or six. His father remarried, had several children by his second wife, and died when Dante was in his teens. At this young age Dante had to take legal charge of the family. This forced him into the precarious world of Florentine public life.

Of his early education we know almost nothing. Typically the local parish priest taught children the basics of reading and writing. The primary texts were the Psalms, Aesop's fables, and teachings of Saint Augustine set in simple verses. Later the Latin poets Virgil, Ovid, and others were studied. The Bible, Augustine, Virgil, and classical mythology left their indelible marks on Dante's spiritual life and writings.

Dante's only recorded personal memory of childhood, documented in his charming "book of memory," *The New Life,* is his encounter with Beatrice when they were both nine years old. She would become Dante's key source of poetic inspiration and the incarnation of all that is good and beautiful in human life. His intense love for her and her premature death at age twenty-four would plunge Dante into an emotional crisis of enormous proportions. Her death would set him on a lifelong quest for the meaning of life and love. It would lead him into a relentless search for truth, goodness, and beauty, down through labyrinthine ways of intellectual pride and moral aberrations to a profound rediscovery of God, whose love, beauty, and goodness Dante first tasted in his early love for Beatrice.

Early Adulthood: A Poet Among Poets

Dante as a young man, before and after Beatrice's death, was a poet above all else. His best friends, like Guido Cavalcanti, were poets, enthusiastically devoted to the "sweet new style" of poetry, whose main themes were the very nature of love and the sublime beauty of the poet's beloved lady. This flowering of romantic poetry had begun in Provence, and soon spread to Sicily and then to the Italian mainland. In Dante's time this poetry of courtly love was extremely popular.

Because it was written in the vernacular, it was more accessible and appealing than poetry presented in classical Latin. At its worst it expressed an almost idolatrous worship of a woman as well as a self-centered quest for emotional satisfaction. At its best, as in the works of Dante, who raised it to its highest expression, it praised a woman's nobility as an incarnation of divine goodness, beauty, and love that could inspire men to the greatest moral and artistic heights. Dante infused this poetry with a depth of spiritual insight drawn from his personal Christian faith and mystical love.

During his early adult years Dante wrote many beautiful love poems while he associated with fellow poets and other kindred spirits, such as the musician Casella and the painter Giotto. Dante intensely loved music and art. Bruni wrote that Dante loved to sing and could draw exceptionally well. Dante noted that God's art is nature and "human art is God's grandchild" (*Inferno* 11:105). Dante's poetry reveals an artist who knew the emotional impact of music and who also appreciated the beauty of form as well as the subtle nuances and symbolic value of color. His creativity as an artistic poet is perhaps unmatched in world literature; the themes of his works—the mystery of God, the mysteries of the universe, the ultimate destiny of all humans beyond this world, the meaning of love—are simply the most sublime and fascinating subjects of human thought and art.

School Years: A Student and Scholar

Dante's insatiable thirst for knowledge drove him to study philosophy and theology in the schools of the Dominicans, Franciscans, and Augustinians in Florence. There he attended lectures by friars who had studied under Saint Thomas Aquinas and Saint Bonaventure in Paris. Both those theological giants considered Saint Augustine the highest authority in theology. Dante studied the works of all three theologians as well as many others. But in the Middle Ages the Bible was the primary and supreme source for theology. Dante's works reveal a thorough knowledge of the Bible, which he cited more than any other book. His second most quoted source was Aristotle, rediscovered with great enthusiasm by medieval phil-

osophers and theologians such as Thomas Aquinas. However, Dante was an original, independent, and eclectic scholar, not an uncritical follower of any one school or authority.

Dante continued his studies at the university of Bologna and later, according to many scholars, at the prestigious university of Paris. While still in Florence he may have been a student of the famous scholar and statesman Brunetto Latini, whom he greatly admired. Brunetto's works deeply influenced Dante's life and works.

Dante's hunger for wisdom embraced every branch of learning: philosophy, theology, and all seven liberal arts. Like many church fathers—including Justin, Origen, and Augustine—he valued the humanistic wisdom of ancient pagan culture. His interests were universal: a passage in *Paradise* even describes a scientific experiment (see 2:94–105). He was truly a Renaissance man a century before the Italian Renaissance. From boyhood to old age he was obsessed with knowing everything knowable. A year before he died he gave a physics lecture in Verona on the topic of water and the earth.

Married Life and Military Service

Dante's father, before his death, had arranged Dante's marriage to Gemma Donati. We know nothing of their union except that they had four children: Peter, James, and John (named after Jesus' closest disciples), and Antonia, who became a poor Clare nun. Boccaccio intimated that the marriage was not happy, but Bruni corrected his innuendos. There is no reason to think it was not a harmonious relationship. We know that Dante's children rejoined him for his final years in Ravenna, but of Gemma we know nothing. His sons Peter and James were the first to write commentaries on Dante's *Comedy.*

While married, Dante, like most Florentine young men, engaged in military service for Florence, which was often at war with neighboring city-states in Tuscany. Dante's vivid descriptions of battles confirm Bruni's words that "Dante, young but well esteemed, fought vigorously, mounted and in the front rank. Here he incurred the utmost peril" (Dinsmore, p. 117). To fill in Boccaccio's gaping silence about Dante's military service, Bruni emphasized that "Dante fought valiantly for his country" (Dinsmore, pp. 117–118). We might find it out of character for such an intellectual and sensitive poet as Dante to be a soldier, but we might also recall that a century earlier Saint Francis of Assisi had been a soldier before his conversion to a life of peacemaking. Francis, an ex-soldier, poet, and peacemaker, would become an inspiring model for Dante.

Public Service

In 1295 Dante entered political life. Public life in Italy during the Middle Ages was a danger zone of almost daily battles between the Guelfs and the Ghibellines, two political parties that supported, respectively, the primacy of the Papacy and the primacy of the holy Roman Empire—though by Dante's time the distinctions between the two parties had become blurred. In general the Guelfs were a rising middle class of merchants, bankers, and artisans who formed powerful independent city-states, which were protected by papal power from the rule of mighty feudal nobles who acted as princes of the empire. In reality the Guelfs were often aristocratic families who controlled local politics in the city-states. Such was the case in Dante's Florence, which was then Guelf. Dante supported the common people rather than the "magnates," the wealthy nobility. Later he would call himself "a party of one," even while he supported the Ghibelline cause in opposition to papal political rule.

Elected to the city council, Dante voted in favor of improving conditions for the poor, such as through hospital and prison reform. He accepted a nonpaying position as streets commissioner in order to make roads safe for the common people. He was genuinely concerned about justice and social reform. However, there may be some truth to Boccaccio's remarks that Dante sought public office for power, fame, and glory. Throughout his life Dante also apparently craved recognition and fame. Perhaps he enjoyed mingling with the aristocrats because he was from a lower social class, or maybe the excitement of public life lured him into its snares and catastrophes. Dante's political career reached its peak when he was elected one of the seven priors, who occupied the highest position under the lord mayor. But disaster soon befell him.

Dante's integrity was the cause of his political downfall. Like Saint Thomas More, he was a good public servant, but a servant first of his conscience, God's voice in his soul. As a council member he had vehemently opposed a proposal to call on papal military intervention to settle the Guelfs' split into two warring factions. Dante was convinced that the pope—Boniface VIII—should not be a worldly ruler with troops to enforce his will. Dante's theological understanding of the papacy saw it as a spiritual authority established by God to guide the world to its eternal salvation. He believed that the pope should use only moral and sacramental means to lead people to their heavenly goal, that God had not given him temporal power.

Dante's opposition to a papal theocracy was adamant and uncompromising. It led directly to his condemnation and banishment from Florence. Dante was correct in regarding Boniface as the one ultimately responsible for his exile. Ironically Dante's faith and theology—which seem so obviously right to us today—caused him to lose his family, property, political career, reputation, and native country. He was falsely accused of graft and other political corruption as well as opposition to the pope. Beginning in 1302 three sentences of exile were promulgated against him, the third being death by fire if he should ever return to Florence. The first sentence was issued while Dante was an ambassador at the papal court of Boniface in Rome, seeking a peaceful settlement of the civil war in Florence.

Exile

During his exile Dante did not become a chronic complainer, consumed by self-pity and bitterness, as Boccaccio asserted. He expressed only twice in his major works a lament over his banishment. In *The Banquet* he wrote:

> Through almost all the regions to which our language extends I have gone a pilgrim, almost a beggar, displaying against my will the wound of fortune, which often is imputed unjustly to the discredit of the one wounded. Truly I have been a boat without sail and rudder, driven to different ports, bays, and shores by that parching wind which painful poverty breathes forth. (1,3:3–5)

The second passage of lament comes from his encounter in Paradise with his ancestor Cacciaguida, who predicts Dante's exile:

> It is willed and already plotted and will soon be brought about by him [Boniface VIII] who devises it in the place where Christ is daily bought and sold. . . . You will leave everything you love most dearly. This is the arrow from the bow of exile which will pierce you first. You will taste how salty is other people's bread, how hard the going up and down other people's stairs. (*Paradise* 17:49–60)

Cacciaguida foresees that Dante will be betrayed by evil men and that another corrupt, political pope, Clement V, will oppose the good, just emperor Henry VII, thus thwarting God's design for world peace. He orders Dante to take this bleak vision to the world, but Dante, "a timid friend to truth," expresses fear that such a message will cost him his life. Cacciaguida reassures him that it at first will prick the consciences of the high and mighty and turn them against him, but "once digested will yield nourishment."

Many scholars consider Dante's exile a blessing in disguise, for it forced him to experience life on earth as an exile and pilgrimage to God, the main theme of *The Comedy*. They speculate that we would not have *The Comedy* if Dante had not been exiled. The nineteenth-century Italian poet Giosuè Carducci remarked that in every Italian town, a statue should be erected to Cante de' Gabrielli, the lord mayor of Florence who signed the first sentence exiling Dante.

Suffering and deprivation, although not the cause of great writing, certainly were the catalyst for some of the greatest Christian literature. Saint Paul's letters from prison, Saint Ignatius of Antioch's letters while a prisoner condemned to a martyr's death, Saint Perpetua's journal written in prison awaiting martyrdom with her infant at the breast—all those writings from the first Christian centuries continue to inspire us. In the sixth century, while in prison awaiting a martyr's death, Boethius—statesman, philosopher, theologian, and poet (much like Dante)—wrote his *Consolation of Philosophy*, a great work that deeply influenced Dante. Dante's exile, though not nearly so harsh as the sufferings of the others just mentioned, was nonetheless a protracted period of intense hardships that moved him to contemplate and articulate the realities of ultimate concern to all humans: God, the meaning of this life, and our final destiny in the next life.

In the early years of his exile Dante wrote a brief, unfinished treatise, *The Eloquence of the Vernacular*, to defend the common language as a worthy vehicle for serious literature and lofty themes. He wrote it in Latin to convince the educated elite—the clerics, lawyers, and doctors—of the nobility of the common language and its capacity to educate the common people, who could not read or understand Latin. Dante stated his purpose in the opening words of the treatise:

> Since I find that no one before me wrote a treatise on the common eloquence and since I regard such eloquence as absolutely necessary for all—not only for men but also for women and little children—I wish in some way to enlighten the perception of those who walk the public squares as if blind and unaware of what lies before them. By the heavenly inspiration of God's Word I will try to do a service to the language of common people not only by drawing water from the cup of my talent but by mixing it with the better source—honey from others—in order to give a sweet mixture of water and honey.

The treatise is important for its ground-breaking manifesto that education and high culture should be accessible to all, regardless of gender, class, and age. It is also a milestone for the study of the history of language. Dante, the philologist and theologian, speculated that the first word uttered by Adam was "God," because the origin of speech is joy:

> There is no joy outside of God and total joy is in God, since God is all joy. Consequently the first human speaker first and before anything else said "God." . . . The Maker, the Source and Lover of perfection, gave with the gift of life every perfection to our first ancestor. It is thus reasonable to assert that God's most noble animal would speak his first word by addressing God himself. (*Eloquence* 1:4–5)

For Dante the common language in its naturalness is closer to the Creator, who by the Incarnation assumed human nature and spoke the common language to common people.

About the same time that Dante wrote his treatise in Latin, he put his convictions about the vernacular in practice by beginning a major work in Italian. In *The Banquet* he shared his knowledge with those unable to attend schools and feast on the great wealth of human and divine wisdom, then available only in Latin. By writing in Italian he hoped "to be of service to a very large number of people—women no less than men, a vast number of both sexes—whose language is not that acquired through education, but through the vernacular" (*Banquet* 1,9:5). Dante never completed his "full-course" banquet, but the four finished books provide rich nourishment from the Scriptures, classical philosophy, and Christian theology. In beautiful poetry and brilliant prose he presented a great feast of wisdom. Several passages from that work are quoted in the meditations of this book.

Dante may have left those two works unfinished because the inspiration for *The Comedy* had come to him. (*The Comedy* was Dante's title for this work; the adjective *divine* was added after his lifetime, and this masterpiece is now commonly referred to as *The Divine Comedy*.) Perhaps for some years the idea had been germinating in his mind. He gave as the "ideal" date of his vision the year 1300, the first Jubilee year, proclaimed by Boniface VIII. Most scholars affirm that he was a pilgrim in Rome for that occasion. His friend Giotto commemorated the pope's proclamation with a fresco, still visible in Rome's cathedral at the Lateran.

Rome's basilicas were refurbished for the event. Many magnificent mosaics, which still dazzle pilgrims today, were executed in the churches. Dante would have contemplated those wondrous depictions of Christ and the saints in glory, Mary crowned queen of heaven, and many scenes from their lives. In the basilica of Saint Peter he would have seen "the face of Christ," imprinted on the famous relic, Veronica's veil. In *The Comedy* he described the crowds and the two-way traffic on the bridge near Saint Peter's (*Inferno* 18:29).

Dante may have experienced a spiritual renewal—a profound conversion—as a pilgrim in Rome. Perhaps this was the seed that developed and blossomed later in *The Comedy*. Pope Boniface VIII had exhorted all Christians to make a pilgrimage to Rome to visit Saint Peter's Basilica and the Lateran cathedral. He promised full pardon to all who confessed their sins there. Chroniclers report that at any one time that year there were over two hundred thousand pilgrims in Rome and that the sacristans in the basilicas had to scoop in the pilgrims' monetary offerings with rakes. One suspects that Boniface's intentions were not purely spiritual.

Two years later Boniface issued his bull *Unam Sanctam*, in which he arrogantly claimed that salvation requires that all human beings be subject to the pope. He insisted that the pope received both spiritual and temporal power directly from God. The pontiff could delegate some worldly rule to the emperor, just as the sun sheds its light on the moon. Dante responded to the papal bull with his Latin treatise *The Monarchy*, in which he argued with convincing proofs from the Bible, philosophy, and history that Christ gave Peter and his successors only spiritual power. He concluded that temporal rule belonged to the Roman emperor, another sun, who received his authority directly from God. Dante's *Monarchy* was a bold, risky contradiction of the pope's claims. The papal curia condemned it to be burned publicly, and later, when the Index of Forbidden Books was established in 1557, Dante's book was among the first on that list. In 1966 Pope Paul VI abolished the Index: Dante's ideas by then had long been accepted as true.

The Comedy

Dante probably began *The Comedy* several years after being exiled. In a letter to his patron Can Grande della Scala, the lord of Verona—one of several Ghibelline princes who offered Dante refuge and support during his exile—he stated that the purpose of *The Comedy* was "to remove those living in this life from the state of misery and lead them to the state of happiness" (*Letter to Can Grande* 15). He revealed that the literal subject of the work is "the state of souls after death" and the allegorical subject is "the human person, who by the exercise of freedom—by good or evil choices—becomes liable to rewarding or punishing Justice" (11).

He then explained allegory and its various levels of meaning. Surprisingly he claimed that his work, like the sacred Scriptures, has four meanings: the literal, the allegorical, the moral, and the anagogical. These four meanings were the traditional senses of the Bible as interpreted by the church fathers and medieval theologians. Dante was thus placing his *Comedy* in the genre of sacred writing, inspired by God. He was convinced that he had received a prophetic message from

God for the church and the whole world. Three times in *The Comedy* he is commanded to write down what he sees and take it to earth: by Beatrice, by Cacciaguida, and by Saint Peter himself.

Dante described his divine inspiration in this way: "I am one who, when Love inspires me, takes notice and then utters words from what He dictates in my heart" (*Purgatory* 24:52–54). Dante may seem to us too presumptuous in making this claim to be God's scribe, but many twelfth- and thirteenth-century "prophet-visionaries," such as Saint Hildegard of Bingen and Mechtild of Magdeburg, made such claims to truth unflinchingly.

In that same letter to Can Grande, after discussing the visions granted to Saint Paul and Ezekiel, Dante wrote:

> But if on account of the sinfulness of the writer the readers should cry out against his claim to have reached such a height of exaltation, let them read *Daniel*, where they will find that even Nebuchadnezzar by divine permission beheld certain things as a warning to sinners. . . . God, "Who makes His sun shine on the good and the evil, and sends rain on the just and unjust," sometimes in compassion for their conversion . . . manifests His glory to evildoers, no matter how evil they may be.

Dante considered himself a sinner for whom God extended compassion by granting visions of hell, purgatory, and paradise for his conversion and for the salvation of other sinners in the world. Often in *The Comedy* Dante refers to his visions as sheer grace granted to him because of his unworthiness. There is no reason to doubt Dante's sincerity about the divine origin of his *Comedy*.

Not only was Dante familiar with the writings of many mystics, such as Saint Augustine, Saint Bernard, and Saint Hildegard, but he also claimed that he too personally received an ineffable vision of God. The question of whether Dante was an authentic prophet and mystic is still debated by scholars. Many conclude that he was indeed an inspired prophet and genuine mystic. Mystical experience is indefinable, but Dante's written testimony, especially in his *Paradise*, seems to express an extraordinary—call it mystical—experience given him by God's grace.

Karl Vossler's words on Dante as a mystic seem to come close to the mysterious truth:

> In comparison with Dante, Augustine, Bernard, and Francis appear as natural, born, professional mystics, while from the stubborn material of the banished Florentine only unhappiness could rouse the holy flame.
>
> There was nothing habitual or professional in Dante's piety. I am inclined to call it occasional mysticism, using the word "occasion" not in the sense of a chance occurrence, but of a concrete experience. What is true of occasional poetry applies also to occasional mysticism; they are both a direct, sincere outpouring of the soul, arising not out of chronic exuberance, but from the momentary need of the heart. So there is nothing priestly or ministerial in Dante's piety, nothing of the virtuoso or of the monk. A pious man, but no saint. The lay spontaneity of Dante's piety . . . sets him apart. . . . Herein Dante is modern, more modern than a modern preacher. (Pp. 81–82)

The banished poet and statesman, driven to near despair and perhaps thoughts of suicide, knew what it was to be an exile "in this valley of tears." Uprooted and homeless he felt more poignantly than most Christians the restless pilgrim state of every Christian. His nomadic wanderings, failures, disappointments, and moral aberrations—his hell—brought him to an almost hopeless "bottom," out of which divine help drew him up to see the "City of God," which restored his hope. His *Comedy* expresses his long, hard spiritual journey to God—from the pit of hell, through the moral progress of purgatory (the reordering of his loves), to a final, unspeakable vision of God, whose love blazed before his eyes and intoxicated him with ecstatic joy.

Final Years

Dante spent his last few years in Ravenna as a guest of Guido da Polenta, the last of the Ghibelline lords who protected and supported him. There he performed diplomatic missions for

Guido and taught. He finished *The Comedy* in the contemplative peace of Ravenna. The majestic Byzantine mosaics in the basilicas there may have inspired the final scenes of the heavenly liturgy in his *Paradise.*

Dante's sons and daughter joined him in those last years. He also enjoyed the friendship of the Franciscan friars at their church of Saint Francis in Ravenna. In 1321, on an unsuccessful peace mission to Venice, he contracted a malaria-like disease. Dante died shortly thereafter in Ravenna and was buried in the Franciscan church, perhaps in the habit as a member of the Third Order.

According to tradition Dante on his deathbed composed his own epitaph in Latin verses. Its final words are, "But a happier lot summoned the poet to a better dwelling place in the stars; and here I am enclosed, Dante, exiled from my shores by Florence, the mother who bore me but who loved me so little." Those words reveal Dante's restless pilgrim soul in search of love all his life. They echo the final words of *The Comedy:* "My desire and will were turned like a wheel, evenly moved by the Love who moves the sun and the other stars." His life had been an arduous journey *per aspera ad astra* (through hard, rough roads to the stars).

Dante's Spirituality

Like all Christian spirituality, Dante's was formed and nourished by God's word in the Scriptures, the sacraments, the communion of saints, and prayer. His was a Christ-centered, incarnational spirituality that embraced and loved the whole universe. It affirmed the divine likeness in all humans as well as the divine presence in all things. These are some characteristics of Dante's spirituality:

A Pilgrim Spirituality

The theme of a Christian's life as a pilgrimage to God dominates Dante's major works, especially *The Comedy.* At the very beginning of that composition he identifies with all of us in "our journey of life" (*Inferno* 1:1). He understood through his own experience that we all take detours and get lost, that we fall and rise along the way. Yet he never lost faith that God was real, present, and powerfully active in his life. He kept hope that God would bring him to final happiness and joy in Paradise.

A Worldly Spirituality

Dante's zealous commitment to the common good of the human community was extraordinary and even heroic. His political activities for justice and peace, his promotion of a united human community under one just monarch, and his mission to reform society consumed almost all his time and energy. Although he met with failure upon failure, he never gave up hope for the world's attainment of peace and justice, the conditions necessary for joy and happiness—God's purpose for human life on earth. Like the classical poets Virgil and Ovid and the Hebrew prophets Isaiah and Micah, he believed in the return of the golden age and the restoration of Edenic peace.

A Courageous Spirituality

A striking characteristic of Dante's life and works is his undaunted courage. In the Florentine political forum he fearlessly defended the rights of the common people over the power of the aristocrats. He opposed papal military intervention in Florence's civil war. He wrote a most daring refutation of the pope's claim to temporal power. That alone made him "an enemy of the Church" and a marked man. His association and friendship with Ghibelline lords, often excommunicated by popes for their opposition to papal rule, compounded the hierarchy's hostility toward him. Dante took great risks for being true to his convictions and he suffered grave penalties for his integrity. He once described himself as "a timid friend to truth," but overcame his fear. He spoke and wrote the truth and made many enemies. He stood alone—a party of one, a lone voice crying in the wilderness for reform of a corrupt church and a decadent society.

A Love-Centered Spirituality

Dante understood God as the love who creates and moves the whole universe to its final perfection. It may seem that God's justice dominates Dante's works, but closer scrutiny reveals that God's merciful love rules. God's justice "wills its own defeat by the fervent love and vibrant hopes of humans . . . and so defeated, it defeats through its own Mercy" (*Paradise* 20:93–99). The pagan Roman emperor Trajan, a spokesman for God's justice in Paradise, exemplifies God's mercy to a pagan who performed one merciful act for a poor widow. Hardened sinners who shed "one measly tear" of repentance at the moment of death are embraced and saved by God (*Purgatory* 5:106). "God's boundless mercy stretches out its arms to anyone who turns to it" (3:123). Dante's God is the love that saves us, but we have to love God and others. All morality, according to Dante, is measured by our love (see 17–18). Our salvation or damnation will be based solely on our love or failure to love. Dante's theology is firmly rooted in Christ's words about this one criterion (see Matthew, chapter 25).

A Lay Spirituality

While Christian spirituality is the same for all—laity, clergy, and religious—there are certain different ways of living the Christian life, depending on one's particular vocation. Dante the layman was a good husband and father and an outstanding public servant. He was also a devout Catholic who attended the eucharistic liturgy as well as the liturgy of the hours. His familiarity with the church's liturgical prayers is remarkable, acquired through frequent practice. He no doubt participated often in the Divine Office sung in the Benedictine monasteries of northern Italy. In a monumental fresco in the Vatican palace—the so-called *Disputa*—Raphael painted Dante the layman among the great doctors and theologians of the church, worshiping Christ present in the Eucharist. Dante was always a loyal son of the church, even when he courageously exercised his prophetic office by calling for reform of corrupt church leaders. His love for the church compelled him, and his love for the world moved him to take action for justice and peace.

Dante and Our Times

Although Dante lived about seven hundred years ago, his life and message can inspire us and enlighten our "postmodern" life with all its ambiguities, doubts, and anxieties. His firm faith, strong hope, and steadfast love endured crises and trials the likes of which most of us have never faced. In spite of so much pain and opposition he remained loyal to a corrupt church and a violent world. What sustained him was his spiritual communion with God, whose faithful love gave him the daily strength, the manna in the harsh desert, to forge on toward the final goal: God, the joy of all human desiring.

✧ Meditation 1 ✧

Our Desire for God

Theme: Every human soul, created innocent and child-like by God, desires to return to the Creator. This desire, implanted by God in the depth of the soul, comes from God's desire to share goodness and joy with all people.

Opening prayer: God, help me to know you, our joyous Creator and final joy.

About Dante

We know little about Dante's childhood and parents. His mother died when he was only five or six. His father remarried, but we are told almost nothing of Dante's stepmother. Then his father died when Dante was twelve or perhaps in his late teens. Orphaned at such an early age, Dante felt a poignant desire for parental love the rest of his life. In his *Comedy*, a spiritual autobiography similar to Augustine's *Confessions*, Dante seems to satisfy his unconscious craving—almost an obsession—to hear himself called son. Many persons he loved and admired meet him on his journey through Hell, Purgatory, and Paradise, and call him by the beloved name of son: his teacher Brunetto Latini, his ancestor Cacciaguida, Saint Peter, and even Adam. But three persons more than all the others are mother and father to him during the journey: Virgil, Beatrice, and Saint Bernard, Dante's main guides on his journey to God.

When, halfway through the journey of his life, Dante gets lost in the dark, terrifying forest of sin, Virgil comes to rescue him. Virgil has been sent by Beatrice, who was sent by the Blessed Virgin Mary, Dante's heavenly mother. Mary, who mediates God's maternal love and saving grace, has set the whole process of Dante's salvation in motion.

Virgil leads Dante through Hell and up Mount Purgatory to the earthly Paradise, where Beatrice becomes Dante's guide, leading him to the heavenly Paradise. Beatrice introduces him to Saint Bernard, who leads him to Mary, who grants Dante the joyful experience of God.

Dante's affectionate, childlike relationship with Beatrice, Virgil, and Bernard throughout the journey reveals on a deeper level the radical, innate desire of all human souls for God, who is love. Beatrice, divine wisdom personified, teaches Dante that God, "the Highest Goodness, breathes forth the human soul directly, filling it with so much love for Himself that it desires Him ever after" (*Paradise* 7:142–144).

Dante expresses his childlike faith in God as Creator of each human soul, in what may be the best poetic (and theological) attempt at the mystery:

> From the fond hands of God, Who loves her even before she exists, the simple little soul comes forth just like a child, all smiles and tears at play, knowing nothing except that, having sprung from her Creator's joy, she turns eagerly to whatever delights her. First she tastes a trivial good and, though deceived, she will pursue it unless a guide redirect her love. (*Purgatory* 16:84–93)

Dante thus perceives himself and every human soul as a simple, innocent child who can easily be led astray by her own natural desire for whatever appears good and delightful. "Faith and innocence are found only in little children; both flee before their cheeks grow hair. . . . The white skin of innocence turns black at the first exposure to the lure of worldly goods" (*Paradise* 27:127–137).

Dante's own experience of lost innocence repeats the experience of every human soul. All humans are like their parents Adam and Eve, created by "that Highest Good Who made them good, to do good, and gave them an earthly Paradise as a pledge of eternal peace. Because they sinned they exchanged their childlike mirth and playful joy for tears and toil" (*Purgatory* 28:91–96).

Dante recovers from his sins after his "tears and toil" and finally reaches the heavenly Paradise, where in the great company of the blessed he sees the innocent children born before and after Christ's coming. Their "smiling faces and childish voices" (*Paradise* 32:47) tell Dante how children are saved by God's gracious love alone, before they have the power of reason, choice, or merit. Dante, who has recovered his childlike innocence through repentance and conversion, finds himself now with innocent children. As he shares in their joy he cannot find words to express it. He is like "an infant who still wets his tongue at his mother's breast" (33:108). Dante has come full circle: from being created an innocent child by God to the final childlike enjoyment of God.

Pause: Do you think of yourself as an innocent child created by God's love? Do your desires sometimes deceive you and lead you astray?

Dante's Words

Every being's highest desire, implanted in it first by nature, is to return to its source. Since God is the source, Who creates our souls in His own likeness, (as it is written: "Let us make humans in our own image and likeness"), the soul desires with the greatest yearning to return to God.

And just as a pilgrim traveling along a road never before taken believes that every house he sees from a distance is the inn, and finding it is not, directs his belief to another, and so on, from house to house until he comes to the inn, so it is with our soul. As soon as it starts out on the new and never yet traveled road of this life, it focuses its eyes on the ultimate goal—its highest good. And so whenever it sees something that seems to have some good in it, the soul believes it may be that highest good.

Since its knowledge is at first imperfect, being still inexperienced and uninstructed, trivial goods seem great, and so it begins to desire them first. Thus we see children set their greatest desire on an apple and then later on a pet bird, still later on fine clothes. Later it desires a horse, then a woman, then moderate wealth, and later greater and greater wealth.

This happens because the soul does not find in any of these what it seeks, but thinks it can find it eventually. . . . Each desirable object stands in front of another as in the shape of a pyramid: the smallest, being the first, covers all the others. It's like the apex of the ultimate desirable one, God, Who is the base and foundation of all the others.

Some people go astray and get lost as on earthly journeys. . . . Good travelers reach their goal and find rest. (*Banquet* 4,12:14–20)

Reflection

We all began the journey of this life as children of human parents. Most of us knew them for many years and experienced their love for us. Some of us were orphaned like Dante early in our life. But as believers we all know by faith that our first parent is God, who out of love created our soul and implanted deep within us an irresistible, aching desire for joy, peace, and rest in God, our source and final home. "Our heart is restless until it rests in you," as Augustine wrote in the first paragraph of his *Confessions*.

Paradoxically our innocent desire to find and enjoy God leads us to make mistakes and wrong choices—down many disastrous detours and dead ends. Our sins ironically express our natural hunger and thirst for the greatest joy and peace, which only God can give. We wander down our chosen "labyrinthine ways" until the "Hound of Heaven" catches up to us and saves us.

Dante was caught and saved after he had strayed from the right road. God's saving grace grasped him through several human channels who guided him back. His beloved Beatrice incarnated for him God's love. She was like Christ, a savior for Dante. She was also like Mary, a loving mother. Virgil was like a father who guided and protected him on the journey through Hell.

We might reflect on the many human guides we have had on our life's journeys: parents, friends, spouse, teachers, and church community. They were our support and even saviors in times of crisis. The cliché "God works through people" expresses profound faith in God's incarnational plan for our salvation. God's parental love works through the many people who have guided us and still guide our restless pilgrim souls toward our final home. God draws us back "with cords of human kindness, / with bands of love" (Hosea 11:4).

✧ We received our biological life, a life that will end, from our human parents. How often do we ponder the ultimate origin of all life and of everything that exists? Reflect on how God's love is now creating us, sustaining us, and providing the grace we need to reach our eternal home.

✧ Think of a personal crisis that caused you to experience utter powerlessness, confusion, fear, and perhaps even despair. How did God work through human channels to save you? How did your faith—a grace from God—sustain you?

✧ Reflect on some detours and wanderings in your spiritual life—perhaps some period of self-absorption or addiction. Is some obstacle still blocking your vision of the greatest Good and leading you astray?

God's Word

In my Father's house there are many dwelling places. If it were not so, would I have told you that I go to prepare a place for you? (V. 2)

I will not leave you orphaned. (John 14:18)

Truly I tell you, unless you change and become like children, you will never enter the kingdom of heaven. (Matthew 18:3)

Closing prayer:

O God, you are my God, I seek you,
    my soul thirsts for you.

. . . .
  . . . your steadfast love is better than life.

(Psalm 63:1–3)

✧ **Meditation 2** ✧

Our Divine Nobility

Theme: All humans possess a marvelous nobility of soul and body because they are created in the image and likeness of God's goodness, beauty, and nobility.

Opening prayer: God, fill me with wonder, awe, and gratitude as I contemplate your noble creatures, the work of your hands.

About Dante

From childhood Dante had an insatiable hunger and thirst for truth and beauty—the irrepressible human desire for God, who is truth and beauty. His young mind was at first nourished by the Psalms, the primary text used then to teach children to read. The future "divine poet" was fed as a child by those beautiful, divinely inspired poems, which so often praise God for the marvels of creation. Later he feasted on the classical Latin poets, especially Virgil, whom medieval Christians considered to have been divinely inspired. As a young man he plunged into an intense pursuit of universal truth in the schools of the religious in Florence, and later at the universities of Bologna and Paris. He fed his soul on the wisdom of Christian theologians such as Thomas Aquinas, Bonaventure, and Augustine, as well as ancient Greek and Latin philosophers such as Aristotle, Plato, Cicero, and many others.

This consuming love for all truth preoccupied Dante his entire life. Boccaccio, a Florentine contemporary, reported that Dante was "possessed by the sweetness of knowing the truth of the things shut up by Heaven, and finding naught else in life more dear than this, he utterly abandoned all other temporal cares, and devoted himself wholly to this alone" (Dinsmore, pp. 75–76). Boccaccio also related an anecdote in which Dante, in Siena, was given a book on philosophy. Dante immediately devoured the book on the spot—lying for three hours on a bench in the public square while a great festival of tournaments, games, loud music, and dancing was celebrated all around him. When asked afterward about the festival, he said he saw and heard nothing.

Later during his exile he wrote to a priest friend in Florence: "Can I not anywhere gaze on the face of the sun and stars? Can I not under any sky contemplate the most precious [literally, "sweetest"] truths without first returning to Florence?" Four months before his death, he went to give a lecture on physics in Verona, where he said, "From my boyhood I have been continuously nurtured by love for the truth."

What were those "most precious truths" Dante contemplated all his life? They were many: God, the created universe, the final destiny of humans. But the truth that most absorbed and fascinated him was how the divine is united with the human. The desire to understand this mystery was the central quest of Dante's works as a whole. He was overwhelmed when he contemplated how God is present in the human. He found this truth proclaimed in the Bible, God's revelation, and also in the works of ancient philosophers and poets that he considered to be the "scriptures of the pagans."

This dazzling truth about the "divinity" of human beings filled Dante with wonder especially when he discovered it in a most personal and concrete way: in a young girl from his own neighborhood—Beatrice. She for Dante was an incarnation of this marvelous truth. Like Christ, God's incarnate wisdom, Beatrice radiated divine goodness, beauty, and nobility. She led Dante to contemplate the whole truth in the final vision of Paradise, where Dante sees "our image" in Christ, the second circle of the Trinity: "My eyes were totally absorbed in it. . . . I yearned to know how our image could fit into that circle and be conformed to it. . . . Then a flash of understanding struck my mind and suddenly its wish was granted" (*Paradise* 33:131–141).

Pause: Do you ponder enough the divine image and likeness within yourself and your fellow human beings?

Dante's Words

Of all the creations of Divine Wisdom, the human being is the most wonderful . . . the body so subtly harmonized, so many organs well integrated. The human creature is so wonderful that it is a daunting challenge even to think about it or express it in words. (*Banquet* 3,8)

Human nobility is like the sky where a rich variety of stars shine: intellectual and moral powers . . . so many naturally good traits, praiseworthy feelings, physical beauty and strength. . . . Because of these diverse qualities and powers united in one being, I dare to assert with confidence that human nobility, considered in its diversity, surpasses angelic nobility, although the latter is more divine in terms of unity. (*Banquet* 4,19)

God, the First Cause, infuses into all creatures divine goodness and gifts. . . . Every created being receives the being of the Divine Nature in some way. . . . The more noble the form the more it contains of that Nature: The human soul, the most noble of these forms generated under the heavens, receives more of the Divine Nature than any other such form. The human soul, through the nobility of its highest power, reason, shares in the Divine Nature in a way similar to an angel. The divine light shines into it as into an angel; philosophers consequently call the human being a divine animal. The human mind is that subtle and most precious part of the soul which is divinity. (*Banquet* 3,2)

Reflection

Dante's words from *The Banquet* on the divine and angelic nature of humans are perhaps surpassed by many passages in his *Comedy.* One such passage reads:

> Divine Goodness, burning within Itself, sparkles forth so that It reveals the eternal beauties [angels and humans], who come directly from God's Being and from then on are eternal. . . . They are wholly free and, thus created, most resemble Him, most please Him. The Sacred Flame, which lights all of creation, burns brightest in what is most like Himself. (*Paradise* 7:64–75)

What an awe-inspiring thought: We are "eternal beauties," sparks from the Divine Flame!

Dante was so impressed by the freedom of our will that he called it "the greatest gift that God in His bounty bestowed in creating us, the gift God cherishes the most, the one most like Himself" (5:18–21). Not even the powerful influences of the planets can overcome it:

> The planets may initiate some of your tendencies, but a light is given you to know right from wrong, and free will, which can still overcome all obstacles if nurtured well. You are free subjects of a greater Power, a nobler Nature that creates your mind, and over this the planets have no control. (*Purgatory* 16:73–81)

Dante's reflections on these many wonderful divine gifts should awaken and stimulate our sometimes dull and inattentive minds to wonder at how "divine" we weak, imperfect human beings really are—even during our earthly pilgrimage. At our final transformation we will become even more splendid and divine. Our glorified bodies, like Christ's, will be luminous, shining like precious jewels, as Dante imagined them in Paradise. A poet closer to our times, Gerard Manley Hopkins, also imagined this:

In a flash, at a trumpet crash,
I am all at once what Christ is, since he was what I am . . .
. . . immortal diamond.

(P. 181)

✧ Go out and look up at a clear night sky. Gaze at the stars—beautiful and without number! Think of the countless parts of your body, each with its own function and beauty, working in harmony with the other parts. Consider the countless powers of your soul: reason, conscience, memory, free will, the ability to love. What wonders!

✧ Revisit Shakespeare's words: "What a piece of work is a man! how noble in reason! how infinite in faculties! in form and moving how express and admirable! in action how like an angel! in apprehension how like a god! the beauty of the world! the paragon of animals!" (*Hamlet,* act 2, scene 2, lines 293–296). Shakespeare and Dante are often considered the two greatest poets of the Western world. Savor their similar thoughts and words on the human being: noble, angelic, godlike, endowed with beauty and infinite powers.

God's Word

When I look at your heavens, the work of your fingers,
    the moon and the stars that you have established;
what are human beings that you are mindful of them,
    mortals that you care for them?

Yet you have made them a little lower than God,
    and crowned them with glory and honor.

(Psalm 8:3–5)

Closing prayer: God, I praise and thank you for the marvelous gifts you have given me. May I see them in all my fellow human beings and come to love all people and you.

The Stages of Our Life

Theme: The divine nobility within us is a dynamic seed that can develop, blossom, and produce fruit—acts of love and justice, which bring peace and happiness to ourselves and others.

Opening prayer: God, may the seed of your likeness within me produce fruit throughout my life.

About Dante

Dante's life was only fifty-six years long—brief by today's expectations—but his contributions to the world, especially by his writings, were enormous and lasting. He was convinced that we humans have *two* ultimate goals (not just one, as the theologians then taught): happiness here on earth, achievable by the exercise of our human powers, and eternal happiness with God, attainable only by the help of divine grace. The "natural grace" within us—the divine likeness that bestows intelligence, freedom, the capacity to love and do good—if put to use, can bring about justice and peace, the conditions for human happiness. For Dante this "divine nobility" is the seed of happiness, and can develop throughout all the stages of human life. It can grow, blossom, and produce the fruit of happiness for ourselves and for the whole human community.

Dante produced all his major written works with this specific purpose: to contribute to the common good and bring happiness to others. At the beginning of his daring treatise on world government he wrote that

> people who do not take the trouble to contribute to the common good fail sadly in their duty. They are not trees by running waters that bear fruit in due season. . . . Since I have often reflected much on this matter and fear I might one day be guilty of burying my talents, I desire not simply to blossom but to bear fruit for the common good by displaying truths that no one else has yet attempted. (*Monarchy* 1:1)

Dante began his *Banquet* with Aristotle's words, "All humans naturally desire knowledge, the perfection of the soul, in which our supreme happiness is found." He then stated his purpose in providing a banquet of knowledge for those deprived of it:

> Since every human is by nature a friend of every other human, he is saddened by any deficiency in the one he loves. . . . And since compassion is the mother of kind action, those who possess knowledge always give generously from their wealth to those who are poor. . . . So, moved by compassion, without forgetting myself, I intend to provide for their lack by offering a full-course banquet. (1,1)

Dante also stated his purpose in writing *The Comedy*, the final fruit of his maturity: "The aim of the whole and of the parts is to remove those living in this life from a state of misery and bring them to a state of happiness. . . . It is not for speculation, but for a practical purpose" (*Letter to Can Grande* 15).

Pause: Is your life productive and fruitful for others? Are you using your natural talents to bring happiness to others?

Dante's Words

Let no one boast by saying: "I have nobility through my family line," because those who possess this grace without the blemish of sin are like gods. God alone bestows it on the soul. . . . Nobility is the seed of happiness, infused by God into the soul. The soul adorned with this goodness does not keep it hidden; it shows it from the first moment it weds itself to the body until the moment of death. In its first stage of life it is docile, gentle, and bashful, adorning its body with the beauty of its harmonious parts. In maturity it is temperate and strong, full of love and praised for courtesy, taking delight only in loyalty. In old age it is prudent, just, and known for its generosity. It rejoices in hearing and speaking well of others. Finally in the fourth stage of life it renews its marriage to God, contemplating the end it awaits and blessing the various stages of life through which it has passed. (*Banquet* 4,3)

Reflection

In the final book of *The Banquet,* Dante gave an extended commentary on the passage just quoted, in which he reflected on the four stages of human life. According to Dante the first stage, adolescence, goes from birth to one's twenty-fifth year; then comes youth (maturity), which extends to age forty-five; early old age and extreme old age follow until one is seventy, the "biblical" age for death.

In the tradition of Ecclesiastes, Dante reflected on the various stages of life, preordained by God: "A time to be born, and a time to die; / a time to plant," and so on (see Ecclesiastes, chapter 3). Each time in life has its unique endowment, perfection, and blessing.

Dante's comments on the two middle stages of life are worth reflecting on:

In maturity one is endowed with perfection and fulfillment so that the sweetness of its fruit may profit both oneself and others. . . . Individual perfection, acquired in maturity, ought to be followed by that perfection which sheds light not just on oneself but on others; a person should open out just like a rose which can no longer stay closed, and the scent, created within, should diffuse itself outward. This should happen in the third stage of life. (*Banquet* 4,27:3–4)

For Dante our full blossoming begins at age forty-five—in "early old age"!

Extreme old age also has its unique blessing:

The soul returns to God, as to the port from which it departed when it set sail on the sea of this life, and it blesses the journey it has completed. Just as a good sailor on approaching port lowers his sails and enters it gently, so we should lower the sails of our worldly affairs and turn to God with our whole mind and heart so that we may come into that port with the utmost gentleness and tranquillity. (4,48:3–4)

Dante described the final stage of life with other meaningful metaphors: the ripe apple that gently detaches itself from its branch and the weary traveler who finally returns home. But perhaps Dante's most beautiful and moving analogy is the beloved soul's return to her spouse, God. To illustrate this Dante gave a surprising example from pagan Roman history: Marcia, the wife of the great statesman Cato. She left him to marry another man, but late in life begged Cato to take her back so that she could die as his wife. He forgave her and renewed their marriage covenant. Dante saw in Cato's noble soul the image of God: "What person on earth was more worthy to represent God than Cato?" He saw in Marcia "the noble soul who turns back to God" (4,28:15)

✧ Do you think of death as a violent assault on your life or as a peaceful return to home, a gentle arrival at port after a stormy sea, a reunion with your loving spouse, God?

✧ Make a list of practical things you do, or should do, to protect and nourish human life in its two extremities—in the unborn and in the very old. Are you involved in pro-life activities, at least by your political vote? Do you look after those who are aged in your family and neighborhood?

✧ Rise early to observe the dawn. Dante described "the beautiful face of dawn whose white cheeks turn red and then age into a golden glow" (*Purgatory* 2:7–9). Think of the unique beauty of each stage of life: the innocence of childhood, the rosy bloom of youth, and the golden glow of old age.

✧ Enjoy the beauty and scent of a rose or some other flower. Reflect on your own ability to emanate beauty and goodness by your kind actions for others.

God's Word

Those whose lives number many years should rejoice in them all. Rejoice while you are young; but be mindful of your Creator in the days of your youth before the days of trouble come, before the sun, moon, and stars are darkened, and desire fails. All must go to their eternal home. The silver cord is snapped and the golden bowl is shattered and the dust returns to the earth and the breath returns to God, who gave it. (Adapted from Ecclesiastes 11:8—12:7)

Closing prayer:

The days of our life are seventy years,
or perhaps eighty, if we are strong;

.　.　.　.　.　.　.　.　.　.　.　.　.

So teach us to count our days
that we may gain a wise heart.

.　.　.　.　.　.　.　.　.　.　.　.

O prosper the work of our hands!
(Psalm 90:10–17)

✧ **Meditation 4** ✧

Human and Divine Love

Theme: Human love has a mysterious, divine dimension. In loving Beatrice, Dante experienced the bliss of God's love for him.

Opening prayer: God, may we see in the human persons who love us and whom we love, reflections of your goodness, beauty, and love.

About Dante

Dante was deeply committed to his vocations as husband, father, scholar, statesman, and diplomat, but he was first and foremost a poet—a poet in love, who celebrated human and divine love. As a young man he wrote copious love poems in the fashionable style of his time, the "sweet new style" of the courtly love poets. Those poets—called also devotees of love or troubadours—composed lavish praises and worship of their "lady," whose mortal beauty they so exalted that many of them later in life repented of their profane love and entered monasteries.

Dante's genius breathed new life into this poetic movement, which had become self-centered and decadent. He transformed romantic love poetry by his own experience of love, which was enlightened and transfigured by his Christian faith.

His experience of love began at the age of nine when he first encountered Beatrice Portinari, a lovely Florentine girl of the same age, whose effect on him would last all his life and dominate all his poetic works. Some years after Beatrice's premature death at age twenty-four, Dante wrote "a book of memory" about his love for her: *The New Life.* This book would have brought Dante lasting fame even if he had not composed *The Comedy.* It is a gem of romantic love poetry and beautiful prose, but is much more than that: it contains the seeds of Christian mystical love that blossomed and came to fruition in his *Comedy.*

What is most remarkable and original about Dante's love for Beatrice is its perception and celebration of the divine in the human—Dante's "magnificent obsession." Beatrice, a real flesh-and-blood girl from his neighborhood, radiated for Dante a "divine" beauty, grace, and love that overpowered him. The effects on him were amazement, bliss, and love. The encounter changed him forever. Even though he was not fully aware, at the time, of all the mysterious dimensions of the experience (who understands at nine—or ninety—the mystery of love?), the impression was deep and lasting. His mature work, *The Comedy,* expresses the full development of that initial experience of love. After many years of reflection Dante realized that God's love, beauty, and grace were incarnate in the human person Beatrice. She, as a living likeness of Christ in Dante's life, loved and saved Dante and led him to God.

Pause: Do you discover and celebrate the divine likeness in your fellow humans?

Dante's Words

She appeared to me at about the beginning of her ninth year and I first saw her near the end of my ninth year. . . . At that moment the spirit of life that dwells in the most secret chamber of the heart began to tremble so violently that even the smallest veins of my body were strangely affected. . . . My spirit was stricken with amazement and I said: "Now your blessedness has appeared." I found her of such noble and admirable dignity that the poet Homer's words suited her perfectly: "She seemed the daughter not of a mortal but of a god." . . . Nine years later the miraculous lady appeared, and passing along a certain street, she turned her eyes to where I was standing very timidly; and with indescribable graciousness she greeted me so wonderfully that I seemed at that moment to behold the whole range of possible bliss. I felt such sweet ecstasy—like a drunken man. (2–3)

The number nine was she herself—that is, by analogy. Since three is the sole factor of nine and the sole factor of miracles is three—the Father, Son, and Holy Spirit, Who are three in one—then this lady was a nine, a miracle whose root is the miraculous Trinity itself. (*New Life* 29)

Reflection

When Dante's *New Life* was first printed in the sixteenth century the censors had deleted or changed his original words about Beatrice, references to his "blessedness" and his "salvation." The ecclesiastical critics found them blasphemous and idolatrous, because only God is our blessedness and salvation. They missed Dante's explicit words that Beatrice is an analogy, a likeness of God. She *was* a miracle: a wonder who reflected the divine gifts present in all human persons.

We all recognize in others divine gifts—goodness, beauty, and love—which so attract us that we fall in love. We experience the blessedness and bliss of loving others and being loved by them. However, this love can become merely a satisfaction of our selfish desires. This "lower" love—incomplete and immature—is really excessive self-love and self-worship.

Dante seems to have gone through a conflict or struggle between this "lower," selfish love (*eros*) and the "greater," selfless love (*agape*, Christian love). Often in *The New Life* he held himself up for ridicule as a lesson or warning to his fellow love poets. He exposed his tears and sighs after Beatrice's death as signs of his pathetic self-pity. He realized that his love for her had degenerated into the self-centeredness of the courtly love poets. However, he overcame his crisis and purified his love.

Human love, in spite of its greatness, beauty, and strength, is always beset with weaknesses, ambiguity, and pitfalls. In his poem "To What Serves Mortal Beauty?" Gerard Manley Hopkins called it "dangerous" (Hopkins, p. 167). It sets the blood dancing—as Dante experienced at his first encounter with the beautiful Beatrice. But it can also lead us to love "God's better beauty, grace" (p. 167). Both Hopkins and Dante, two truly Christian poets, perceived that human beings and human love are best understood through faith in the Incarnation. Just as Christ is the human way to the Father, so the beautiful face and eyes of Beatrice led Dante all the way to God. In the words of another Hopkins poem:

As kingfishers catch fire, ...

· · · · · · · · · · ·

[The graced human person *is* Christ]
　　. . . For Christ plays in ten thousand places,
Lovely in limbs, and lovely in eyes not his
　　To the Father through the features of men's faces.

(P. 129)

✧ Look attentively at the faces, especially the eyes, of those close to you. Dante was fascinated by the human face and in particular by the eyes, "the windows of the soul, where she reveals herself most clearly" (*Banquet* 3,8:10). He described Beatrice's eyes as "emeralds from which Love shot loving darts" at him. He saw in her eyes a reflection of Christ, like sunlight in a mirror (*Purgatory* 31:115–123). Reflect on the beauty and brightness in the eyes of those who love you. See in them a reflection of divine Love.

✧ Revisit an album of family photographs. Savor the beauty of its old and young faces—how they reflect, dimly or brightly, something of God's beauty, goodness, and love.

✧ Magazine covers usually feature only the "pretty faces," the superficial "mortal beauty," which holds the most interest for most people. Do you look beyond that and value more the goodness and beauty of human souls, whose faces may not measure up to the current canons of glamour and beauty?

God's Word

Let us love one another, because love is from God; everyone who loves is born of God and knows God. Whoever does not love does not know God, for God is love. . . . No one has ever seen God; if we love one another, God lives in us, and his love is perfected in us. (1 John 4:7–12)

Closing prayer: God, you revealed your love for us through Jesus, human and divine. Grant us the happiness of loving you through our love for our human brothers and sisters.

✧   **Meditation 5**   ✧

Loss and Grief

Theme: Grief over the loss of a loved one, in itself natural and wholesome, can lapse into morbid self-pity. Christian faith heals and transforms it.

Opening prayer: God of all consolation, enlighten our heart to see your saving purpose in death.

About Dante

Beatrice's death plunged Dante into a crisis so profound that he responded to that crisis in one form or another for the rest of his life. However, that crisis transformed Dante into a profoundly Christian poet. Dante told the story of the crisis and transformation in *The New Life,* essentially an account of how his grief and near despair were radically changed by the intervention of Christian faith.

Dante unabashedly poured out his grief, tears, and morbid sighs in *The New Life,* mentioning no fewer than twenty-two sighs. He compared himself to Jeremiah, weeping and lamenting over the destruction of Jerusalem, left widowed, alone, and desolate. Dante's heart was torn apart and bleeding, like the young Augustine's after the death of his closest friend (see Augustine's *Confessions,* bk. 4). He found consolation only in tears and sickly sighs. His life had become so empty and meaningless that he desired death. Boccaccio reported that "by [Beatrice's] departure Dante was thrown into such sorrow, such grief and tears, that many of those nearest him, both relatives and friends, believed that death alone would end them. They expected that this would shortly come to pass" (Dinsmore, p. 80).

Then Dante experienced a breakthrough—a divine intervention in the form of inner visions. He saw Beatrice's death accompanied by the same signs present at Christ's death: the darkened sun, women weeping, violent earthquakes. Her death occurred at the ninth hour, the hour of Christ's death. After this vision came another in which he saw a multitude of angels following a pure white cloud (Beatrice's soul) into heaven, as they sang, "Hosanna in the highest." The scene evoked Christ's Ascension and Mary's Assumption.

Those visions did not immediately remove all his grief. One day he met some pilgrims passing through Florence on their way to Rome to gaze on the face of Christ, miraculously impressed on Veronica's veil. They were far from home and missed their loved ones left behind. Dante addressed a sonnet to them, inviting them to weep with him over *his* loss of Beatrice. Such arrogance and sick self-pity! After recovering from this last fit of self-indulgence, he wrote the final sonnet of *The New Life,* part of which is quoted in the next section of this meditation. His final sigh was now healthy and faith filled—a pilgrim's sigh, capable of ascending to heaven.

Pause: Has your grief over the loss of a loved one become morbid, self-centered, and devoid of hope?

Dante's Words

Beyond the highest sphere of heaven, passes the sigh that comes from my heart; a new understanding that Love in tears placed within it, urging it on high. Once arrived at the place of its desiring it sees a lady held in reverence, splendid in light; and through her radiance the pilgrim spirit looks upon her being.

After I wrote this sonnet there came to me a miraculous vision in which I saw things that made me resolve to say no more about this blessed one until I would be capable of writing about her more worthily. To achieve this I strive as much as I can, and this she truly knows. And so, if it be the pleasure of Him through Whom all things live that my life continue for some years, I hope to write of her what has never been written of any other woman. Then may it please the One who is Lord of graciousness that my soul go to see the glory of its lady, that blessed Beatrice, who in glory contemplates the face of the One "Who is through all ages blessed." (*New Life* 41–42)

Reflection

The death of Beatrice, the central memory in *The New Life*, took on an entirely new meaning for Dante once he placed it within the central memory of Christian faith: the death and Resurrection of Christ. Dante now found salvation in Beatrice's death. The God of love had placed a new understanding in his heart. His regenerated faith now understood her death as grace in the midst of disgrace. Beatrice's mortal beauty, her unique personhood, her brief life and tragic death were not in vain, for she had entered a new eternal life and was now gazing on the face of Christ, "Who is God, through all ages blessed" (*New Life* 42).

These final words of *The New Life* mark the beginning of Dante's "new life." From now on Beatrice, glorified in Christ, would love and inspire him even more. She would help him through later crises. Like Christ she would even "descend into hell" to save him. Beatrice's love for Dante (and his love for her) would draw his pilgrim spirit all the way up to enjoy with her the beatific vision of God.

✧ At the eucharistic liturgy we all proclaim and sing the central memory of our faith: "Christ has died, Christ is risen, Christ will come again," or something similar. Does this memory transform your sad memories of lost loved ones and change your understanding of death?

✧ Visit or telephone someone who is grieving. Share your sincere Christian faith and hope with that person rather than repeat trite platitudes about time healing all wounds.

✧ Contemplate a Byzantine icon of Christ's Resurrection. Such icons depict his descent into "hell," the dark prison of death. They show the refulgent Christ with his cross in one hand, grasping the hands of Adam and Eve and leading them and the Old Testament saints up to heaven. Dante would have often contemplated this scene, common in the medieval churches of Italy. Reflect on the meaning of Christ's death on the cross for you, and his promise and power to raise you up to eternal life with himself and your loved ones.

God's Word

We do not want you to be uninformed, brothers and sisters, about those who have died, so that you may not grieve as others do who have no hope. For since we believe that Jesus died and rose again, even so, through Jesus, God will bring with him those who have died. . . . For the Lord himself . . . will descend from heaven, and the dead in Christ will rise first. Then we who are alive, who are left, will be caught up in the clouds together with them to meet the Lord in the air; and so we will be with the Lord forever. Therefore encourage one another with these words. (1 Thessalonians 4:13–18)

Closing prayer:

Dying you destroyed our death,
rising you restored our life.
Lord Jesus, come in glory.
(Memorial Proclamation of Faith II)

✧ **Meditation 6** ✧

Joy in God's Creation

Theme: The universe is a wonderful work of art, a garden of delights, created by God, the artist and gardener. It intoxicates us with joy and fills us with love and praise for its Creator.

Opening prayer: God, supreme artist and gardener, may we love and praise you for every leaf in this garden of the universe.

About Dante

During his years in exile Dante wrote, "I traveled through almost all the regions to which our language reaches, a homeless wanderer, reduced almost to beggary" (*Banquet* 1,3:4). After some fifteen years of exile he wrote to a friend in Florence, "Can I not anywhere gaze upon the face of the sun and stars without first returning to Florence?" (*Epistle XII* 9). During those years of wandering, Dante would have traveled by foot or on a horse or mule at a slow pace, exposed to all the splendors of the earth, sea, and sky. Those nineteen years of travel through Italy, one of the most beautiful and scenically diverse countries in the world, brought him into close contact with the grandeur and diversity of God's creation. Dante called Italy "the garden of the Empire, the most noble region of Europe."

In his *Comedy*, written during that period, he not only keenly observed all facets of nature but often endowed them with personal traits and moods: "The morning star, Venus, makes the whole eastern sky smile" (*Purgatory* 1:9). Nature's smile was contagious for Dante: "I seemed to see the whole universe turn into a smile, and through my eyes and ears I drank in divine inebriation" (*Paradise* 27:4–7).

During his last years Dante often frequented the beautiful pine forest near Ravenna. It was perhaps there that he was inspired to write his unforgettable description of the earthly paradise, the Garden of Eden (see *Purgatory* 28). In that Paradise the gentle breeze, the trees, and the birds all join in a joyful symphony to welcome the dawn. Dante encounters a beautiful lady gathering flowers that "paint her path." She is Matelda (perhaps representing the medieval mystic Mechtild of Magdeburg, who also described the earthly paradise). Matelda radiates the joy of a woman in love as she smiles and sings words from Psalm 92: "You have delighted me, O Lord, by your work. I sing for joy at the works of your hands."

Matelda echoes the "childlike mirth and playful joy" of Adam and Eve in that first garden, the nest and cradle for humans and pledge of their eternal home. The whole scene reminds Dante of the ancient myth of Proserpine gathering spring flowers in a meadow in Sicily. Springtime in Sicily epitomized for the classical poets the pristine golden age of human happiness. Dante may have enjoyed a spring in Sicily, still a delightful experience for the traveler there today.

Dante's enjoyment of God's garden here on earth was not merely an aesthetic experience. It moved his heart to love God, the gardener. When Saint John in Paradise questions his motives for loving God, Dante responds: "The being of this world and my own being, the death He died that I might live. . . . brought me to true love. I love each leaf with which all the garden of the Eternal Gardener is enleaved in measure of the good He gives to each" (*Paradise* 26:63–66). For Dante this world is a garden, but the heavenly Paradise is an even more beautiful garden where the saints are like garlands of flowers, dancing and singing joyfully. The whole company of the blessed is a splendid white rose basking under the light and warmth of God, their sun. The Triune God is the great light of three circles radiating the colors of the rainbow. Dante's God and universe are all light and colors that cause intoxicating joy. Dante sees how the Great Light "contains within its depths all things bound in a single book by Love, of which creation is the scattered leaves" (33:85–87).

Pause: God has placed us in an earthly paradise. Does the beauty and grandeur of this garden fill you with joy and love for its Creator?

Dante's Words

Looking upon His Son with the Love which the One and the Other eternally breathe forth, the uncreated, ineffable Power made everything that moves in mind and space with such sublime order that whoever sees it cannot help tasting Him.

Look up now, reader, with me to the lofty spheres and lovingly contemplate the work of that great Artist Who so loves His art that His eyes never turn from it. (*Paradise* 10:1–12)

Reflection

Dante perceived that the eternal love of the three Divine Persons—their inner life as a community of love—is the power that flows outward, creating the universe in space and time. Just as the mutual love of the Father and the Son breathes forth the Spirit, so God's love breathes forth the universe. So when we contemplate the sublime order and beauty of the universe, we can experience God's power and love—we can "taste" God! God's loving eyes never turn away from God's art; when we turn our eyes to it we see and taste God's love.

The order and beauty of this world delighted Dante and can delight us too. This garden is our cradle and nest, a temporary home to be loved and cared for, but it is still merely a pledge or first installment of an even greater, eternal home predestined for us.

God has created an order in the universe, wherein "all beings move to a different port across the vast ocean of being—each endowed with its own instinct as guide" (*Paradise* 1:3). All creatures find their rest and peace in their natural home, their predestined placed in God's harmonious universe. "Some plants thrive on mountains, others sing, as it were, when alongside water" (*Banquet* 3,2:3). Creatures endowed with intellect, free will, and immortality—the angels and humans—are predestined and directed by the Divine Archer for the happy target of an eternal home with God, where they will sing for joy when they find their perfect rest and peace.

✧ Go into a garden, a park, or open country and enjoy the vast variety of beauties—sky, trees, birds, and flowers—all the leaves of the cosmic garden. Taste the beauty, power, and love of the Eternal Gardener.

✧ Read, contemplate, and pray the words of Psalm 104, a moving poem in praise of God the Creator.

✧ Read and enjoy Gerard Manley Hopkins's poem "God's Grandeur." Savor the final lines comparing the dawn to God's Holy Spirit, who "with warm breast and with ah! bright wings"—like a mother bird—broods over the world every day (p. 128).

✧ Do you cherish and take care of this earthly paradise as a home shared with many other creatures? Are the plants, animals, air, water, and earth your sisters and brothers? Are you aware that God's command to dominate and rule all other creatures is properly understood as a command to imitate God's rule, which is nurturing and providential rather than exploitative and greedy? Talk about these matters with a trusted friend.

✧ Dante, like Francis of Assisi, Mechtild of Magdeburg, Hildegard of Bingen, and many other medieval mystics, praised God with joyful songs. Does your parish liturgy express this joy? What might you do to help make such expression happen?

God's Word

People were so delighted by the beauty of these things—the luminaries of the sky, the fire, wind, storms, the circling stars and rushing waters—that they thought these things must be gods. Let people know how much greater than these is their Lord, the author of beauty who created them. People are so amazed at the power and activities of these things; let people perceive from them how much more powerful is the One who made them. When we realize how vast and beautiful creation is, we learn about the Creator at the same time. (Adapted from Wisdom of Solomon 13:1–5)

Closing prayer: O God, my soul rejoices in the wonderful works of your hands. I praise you for this foretaste of the eternal joy you have prepared for us.

Smiles and Laughter

Theme: Smiles and laughter are the shining glass that reveals the soul's inner joy; the best joy has the light and color of love.

Opening prayer: Fill my soul, God, with your love and joy; let it shine on others through smiles and laughter.

About Dante

Boccaccio noted that Dante's "complexion was dark, his hair and beard thick, black, and curled, and his expression ever melancholy and thoughtful" (Dinsmore, p. 95). He then related an anecdote about Dante, whose fame as the author of the *Inferno* was so widespread that people everywhere knew him at sight. One day in Verona Dante passed a group of women and overheard one say to the others: "Do you see the man who goes down into hell and returns when he pleases, and brings back tidings of them that are below?" Another replied: "You must indeed say true. Do you not see how his beard is crisped, and his color darkened, by the heat and smoke down there?" On hearing these words Dante smiled a little and walked on (p. 96).

A later biographer, Leonardo Bruni, who often corrected Boccaccio's gossipy version of Dante's life, described Dante's face as "pleasant but deeply serious" and referred the reader to an excellent portrait of Dante in the Church of Santa Croce in Florence (Dinsmore, p. 126). No portrait is there today, but there are two portraits of Dante in Florence: one attributed to his friend Giotto, and another by Nardo di Cione (circa 1357). Both show Dante with a pleasant, peaceful face among the blessed in Paradise.

It seems that Boccaccio's "ever melancholy" Dante and Bruni's "pleasant" Dante describe two sides of the man: he was melancholy when he experienced so much evil and misery in this world and then saw the sad end of evil souls in Hell; he was pleasant when he experienced goodness and happiness here and saw the joy of the blessed in Paradise.

Boccaccio conceded that Dante smiled once—but just a little. According to Boccaccio, Dante had serious defects—chronic bitterness, rage, and lust. The biographer mentioned these faults, though fearful of tarnishing the reputation of such a great man, and hastily begged pardon of Dante, "who perchance, while I am writing this, looks down at me with scornful eye from some high region of heaven" (Dinsmore, p. 102).

Bruni's Dante was not chronically bitter, angry, or lustful: "He delighted in music and singing, and drew exceedingly well. . . . In his youth he associated with young lovers, and he, too, was filled with a like passion, not through evil desire [as Boccaccio had asserted], but out of the gentleness of his heart" (Dinsmore, p. 126). Dante's writings confirm this portrait, revealing a man who found great joy in life, who sang, smiled, and laughed with his friends as they enjoyed love, music, and art together. He experienced joy on earth as well as a foretaste of heavenly joy with God and the blessed.

Pause: Is your life joyful: do you laugh, sing, and love enough?

Dante's Words

In Dante's time the Italian word for smile *(sorriso)* had the same meaning as the word for laughter *(riso)*. Dante gave us a stupendous definition of smile and laughter:

The soul reveals itself in the mouth like color behind glass. And what is laughter if not a flashing forth [the Italian *corruscazione* means "flashing, shining, sparkling"] of the soul's delight: a light appearing externally, which corresponds to the state of being within. (*Banquet* 3,8:11)

But here we do not repent. We smile instead: not at the sin—this does not come to mind—but at the Power that orders and provides.

From here we gaze upon that art which works with such effective love; we see the Good by which the world below returns above. (*Paradise* 9:102–108)

Reflection

The speaker of the verses just quoted from *Paradise* is a soul in the sphere of Venus: Folquet, a French troubadour, known for his many amorous affairs. He has repented, and become a Carthusian monk and then a bishop. His smile now expresses the joy of his fellow "children of Venus"—those once overcome by the power of erotic love, but now dancing, singing, and sparkling like jewels. Next to Folquet shines Rahab, the whore of Jericho. They all smile, not at their sins but at God's love, goodness, and power—God's providential art—which forgave them and brought them from Earth to Paradise.

In Purgatory too the souls often smile. There Dante meets Manfred, a notorious sinner on Earth—twice excommunicated—who smiles as he tells Dante that at the moment of death he turned to God, who forgave and saved him: "Horrible were my sins, but boundless Mercy has such wide arms that He receives all who turn to Him" (*Purgatory* 3:121–123).

But it is in Paradise that smiles and laughter abound. All the blessed "are wrapped by their sweet love in a mantle of smiles" (*Paradise* 20:13–15). Why do the blessed smile? They radiate the joy of being "in God." All in Paradise—from the least forgiven sinners to the highest seraphim—are so filled with God's love and joy that they are "ingodded." This is one of Dante's many word inventions in Paradise, and it attempts to express the inexpressible—our final divinization. What God is we will become and are already becoming!

And what is God? Dante's final description of the Trinity is his most extraordinary and most untranslatable tercet: "O Light Eternal, Who alone dwells in Yourself, alone knows Yourself, and known to Yourself, loves and smiles on Yourself" (33:124–126). God's "self" is the inner circling of the Father and Son, who know and love each other. Their love is the Holy Spirit, the smile of the Trinity. Therefore the blessed, "ingodded" into the divine circling of love, smile. Dante too smiles as he sees God's smile "turn the whole universe into a smile" (27:5).

✧ The fruit of the Holy Spirit is love, joy, and peace (see Galatians 5:22). Does your face show that fruit often enough with a sincere smile?

✧ Gilbert K. Chesterton ended his book *Orthodoxy* with the words, "There was some one thing that was too great for God to show us when He walked upon our earth; and I have sometimes fancied it was His mirth." True, the Gospels are silent about Jesus' smiles and laughter, but I fancy he did smile and laugh. Make a list of Gospel passages where you fancy Jesus would have smiled or laughed.

✧ Modern medical professionals have confirmed the ancient wisdom that laughter benefits one's health. Try to bring some laughter to people who are sick. Watch with them the film *Life Is Beautiful* or *Patch Adams.* Let Roberto Benigni or Robin Williams make them and you laugh.

✧ The souls in Dante's *Inferno* neither smile nor laugh. They have rejected and thus lost God, the source of joy. But Dante provided for us readers some comic relief in that joyless place. Read and enjoy canto 21—a delightful farce peppered with vulgar four-letter words. Some Italian editions delete those words; Italian teenagers love the original!

God's Word

As the Father has loved me, so I have loved you; abide in my love. . . . I have said these things to you so that my joy may be in you, and that your joy may be complete. (John 15:9–11)

Closing prayer:

Let me hear joy and gladness;
    let the bones that you have crushed rejoice.

. . . .

Do not cast me away from your presence,
    and do not take your holy spirit from me.

(Psalm 51:8–11)

✧ Meditation 8 ✧

Sin: Our Dark Side

Theme: Deep within us all lurk dark, powerful tendencies to sin. If unchecked they can wreak havoc and cause unspeakable pain and misery.

Opening prayer: God, grant me the courage to confront honestly my sins and evil inclinations.

About Dante

Dante held optimistic views on the goodness of human nature, the divine nobility of the soul, and the soul's fruitful development through the various stages of life. He thought that the highest point of that development—the zenith of the arc of our life span—occurs between the years of thirty and forty, midway through the "biblical" life expectancy of seventy or eighty years. That is why Christ, endowed with a perfect human nature, chose to die in his thirty-fifth year (see *Banquet* 4,23:10–11).

Yet when Dante reached that midpoint he experienced not the zenith of his potential but instead the lowest point of weakness—utter powerlessness and loss of self. He described this misery in the first canto of the *Inferno*, where he is lost in a dark, terrifying forest, a wild, deserted place. In an attempt to escape from it he encounters three beasts—a lion, a leopard, and a wolf—which block his way. All three are metaphors expressing his emotional and moral turmoil: his isolation, fear, and helplessness as he confronts the evil beasts within himself—the deadly sins of pride, lust, and avarice.

Terrified, he turns back, but sees a shadowy figure coming toward him. Dante cries out, "Have mercy on me"—his first words in *The Comedy*. The figure is Virgil, who tells Dante that he must take another way in order to escape the beasts. The other way will be a journey through Hell. He tells Dante that the beasts are so powerful that only the Greyhound—a savior endowed with wisdom, love, and power—can destroy them.

Pause: Has some crisis in your life brought you to helplessness, lostness, and a horror of your sins?

Dante's Words

Midway through the journey of our life
I woke to find myself in a dark wood,
for I had lost the right path.

How hard it is to tell what it was like:
this wood, so wild, rough, and harsh
the very thought of it renews my fear.

It is so bitter that death is hardly more so.
But to show the good that came of it
I will tell of things other than the good.

(*Inferno* 1:1–9)

Reflection

Dante identified with all of us in *our* journey through life. Halfway through that journey he wandered off the right path and got lost. We cannot know with certainty the exact nature of his sins, but pride, lust, and covetousness, the chief deadly sins, are the deep roots of his and our aberrations. All his wrong choices and sins came back with a blast to strike him down. He was forced to face his own dark self, to notice all the lost parts of his life, to travel backward and downward into the neglected corners of his soul, the ugly, hidden secrets of his past and present. The terrifying journey into self-knowledge!

To face one's awesome weaknesses—one's nothingness— is at first a humbling and most horrifying experience. Dante was overwhelmed when he discovered that he had no control over those forces within himself. He cried out for help. In his masterful record of his spiritual journey, Virgil is sent by Mary, Lucy, and Beatrice—a human, maternal trinity—to help him. Virgil gives Dante hope for final salvation by the divine Trinity of Power, Wisdom, and Love.

Virgil leads him down through Hell, where Dante sees the consequences of sin. All the characters in Hell are really present in Dante's own soul. He sees himself in them. They are not so much being punished for their sins as they are suffering the consequences of their free choices. They get what they desired. Uncontrolled, misdirected desires are at the root of sin. Dante learns to follow his own misguided desires down to their bitter end. The journey through Hell is the education of his desires. That is the "good" he finds there—the grace in Hell. His vision of Hell is the first step out of his personal hell—tough and bitter, but necessary for his salvation.

✧ Dante did not journey through the hell of his sins alone. He had help and direction, both human and divine. Reveal to a spiritual friend or your confessor some hidden weakness, inclination, or sin that you have feared facing. Find grace in self-knowledge and self-revelation.

✧ If someone you know is going through an emotional, moral, or spiritual crisis, offer that person courage and hope by your presence and gentle words of support and guidance.

✧ Spiritual wisdom from all traditions teaches us the necessity of self-knowledge. Do you examine your conscience at the end of the day?

God's Word

There is no health in my bones
    because of my sin.
For my iniquities have gone over my head;
    they weigh like a burden too heavy for me.

My wounds grow foul and fester
    because of my foolishness;
. . . .
I am utterly spent and crushed;
    I groan because of the tumult of my heart.

O Lord, all my longing is known to you;
    my sighing is not hidden from you.

(Vv. 3–9)

Do not forsake me, O LORD;
　　O my God, do not be far from me;
make haste to help me,
　　O Lord, my salvation.

(Psalm 38:21–22)

Closing prayer: "God, be merciful to me, a sinner!" (Luke 18:13).

✧ **Meditation 9** ✧

Pride: Diseased Self-Love

Theme: The deepest root of all our sins is pride: a diseased self-esteem and self-love.

Opening prayer: God, help me to see clearly the truth about myself. Heal my sick self-love.

About Dante

Dante was a proud man. He candidly admitted that pride was his most besetting sin. After going through the first level of Purgatory, the purging of pride, he reflects with great fear and trembling on the heavy, long penance he will have to endure there after his death (*Purgatory* 13:136–138). On that first terrace of Purgatory he meets souls purifying themselves of three kinds of pride: pride in nobility of blood, pride in one's talents, and pride in worldly power. All three prides are also in Dante. The souls in Purgatory, like those in Hell, represent what is within Dante's own soul.

Although Dante often wrote that true nobility is not something inherited from one's ancestors, he nonetheless took great pride in his nobility of blood as a great-great-grandson of Cacciaguida, knighted by the emperor for his valor in the Second Crusade. Cacciaguida died as a Christian martyr in the Holy Land. When Dante meets Cacciaguida in Paradise, Cacciaguida informs him that Alighiero, Cacciaguida's son and Dante's great-grandfather, has been on the first level of Purgatory for more than a hundred years. Pride seems to be a family sin! Dante, in the awesome presence of his most noble ancestor, is overcome by pride, for which he quickly reproaches himself: "Oh, our petty pride in noble blood! It will never again amaze me that you make people glory in you here on earth, where our affections are weak, for up there in Heaven itself, where appetites are not warped, I gloried in my blood" (*Paradise* 16:1–6).

Numerous passages in *The Comedy* confirm reports that Dante took great pride in his talents. In Limbo the greatest poets of antiquity—Homer, Virgil, Ovid, Horace, and Lucan—welcome him as an equal into their elite "noble circle" (*Inferno* 4:99–102). Even in Paradise Dante expresses more than once his desire and expectation to be crowned poet laureate in Florence (*Paradise* 1:26; 25:7).

Dante's involvement in the political arena may also have been motivated to some extent by a desire for power and glory. Boccaccio, after praising Dante's devotion to public service, added that Dante was enticed "by the sweetness of glory, by the empty favor of the populace" to "pursue the fleeting honor and false glory of public office" (Dinsmore, p. 87).

Pause: Do different kinds of pride warp your motives, affections, and appetites?

Dante's Words

O proud Christians, wretched, sluggish souls,
all you whose inner vision is diseased,
putting your trust in things that pull you backward,

are you not aware that we are worms,
each born to form the angelic butterfly,
that flies defenseless to the Final Judge?

Why do your soul's pretensions rise so high,
since you are still only defective insects,
worms as yet imperfectly evolved?

(*Purgatory* 10:121–124)

Reflection

These words of Dante may seem harsh and preachy, but he includes himself with all of us. We are all defective worms at present, but we are also destined for a wonderful transformation into an angelic butterfly. The strong, earthy metaphor of a worm expresses well our present, undeveloped, imperfect condition, from which we can grow into something marvelously beautiful—a butterfly capable of flying to God.

Dante sees the souls on the first ledge of Purgatory learning humility by carrying heavy stones that force them down to the earth, the humus from which they came. They learn humility also by reciting an appropriate prayer—the Lord's Prayer—which Dante has paraphrased and adapted to their need to purge their love and worship of self, the diseased vision of themselves as the center of the universe.

In their prayer (*Purgatory* 11:1–24) they address God as *our* (not *my*) Father, who is in Heaven with his highest creatures, the angels. They then praise God's power and give thanks for God's "sweet outpouring" of gifts. They ask that the peace of God's Kingdom come to them, because they cannot attain it by themselves. They offer their will as a sacrifice to God, just as the angels do. They beg for daily manna through their desert journey. They ask forgiveness of God, as they forgive those who wronged them. And finally they pray for deliverance from the Evil One, but add that this last request is not for themselves, but for those still on Earth. Their self-love is indeed being transformed into love for others.

✧ Recite slowly and reflect on the Lord's Prayer, a perfect expression of humility, which is essentially the truth about ourselves. Notice in the first part our recognition and praise of God, whose paternal love is the power that rules over us and the whole universe. In the second part we make three simple requests for our basic needs: food, forgiveness, and protection from evil. We thus become wholesomely dependent on God as our sick vision of self is healed. We even become like God, as we forgive others. This prayer transforms us.

✧ Dante humbly acknowledged his great poetic talent as a gift from God. He referred to his *Comedy* as "this sacred poem to which both Heaven and Earth have set their hand." Think about your gifts and talents. Praise and thank God for them; use them for the benefit of others.

✧ Popular culture today idolizes self-esteem. Perhaps we should heed Dante's truthful perception that "no one is capable of measuring his or her own worth truly and justly, so much does self-love deceive us" (*Banquet* 1,2:8). Do you try to balance a healthy recognition of your gifts with an equally wholesome awareness of your defects?

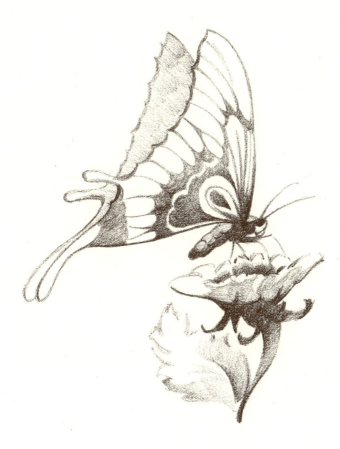

God's Word

"God opposes the proud,
    but gives grace to the humble."
Submit yourselves therefore to God. Resist the devil, and
he will flee from you. Draw near to God, and he will
draw near to you. Cleanse your hands, you sinners, and
purify your hearts, you double-minded. . . . Humble
yourselves before the Lord, and he will exalt you. (James
4:6–10)

Closing prayer: God, grant me humility to see and accept
the whole truth about myself: your many good gifts to me and
my many imperfections.

Peace and Justice

Theme: A basic responsibility of all human persons is to contribute to the common good of this world. Peacemaking and doing justice are fundamental duties for all of us.

Opening prayer: God, make me an instrument of your peace!

About Dante

Throughout his adult life Dante was passionately committed to justice and peace for his city, Florence, for his nation, Italy, and for the whole world. As a young man he was active in public service to his city. Elected to the council, he voted for reforms of the Ordinances of Justice to benefit the poor. He supported hospital and prison reform, and even served without salary as streets commissioner to make the roads accessible and safe for the common people.

Florence then was in turmoil: powerful wealthy families constantly feuded with one another for control. The conflicts were so violent that one faction called on papal troops to bring peace. Dante, in council, vehemently opposed this use of papal power. Ironically, while in Rome as an ambassador to the pope to seek a peaceful settlement, he was sentenced to exile by the faction in power.

During his exile he continued to serve as an ambassador for the princes of northern Italy, always at war with one another. In his anguish over his country's plight he cried out:

Ah, slavish Italy, home of grief, ship without pilot caught in a raging storm, no queen of provinces—but a brothel! No one within your bounds knows rest from war and even those enclosed by the same wall and moat are at each other's throats! O miserable Italy, can you find within you any part that is at peace? (*Purgatory* 6:75–87)

The pilot, according to Dante, should be not only king of Italy but ruler of the whole world—the holy Roman emperor. This ruler should be both just and charitable—a "servant of all," whose unselfish service and authority could bring about the peace necessary for human happiness, God's providential design. In his treatise *The Monarchy* Dante proposed and defended his vision of universal peace and justice.

Pause: Do you contribute some time and energy in service to your local community?

Dante's Words

Since human beings share in both corruptibility and incorruptibility, they are the only beings ordered toward two ultimate goals. . . . Divine Providence has set them to attain these two goals: first, happiness in this life and second, happiness in eternal life. . . . This is why two guides have been appointed for them to lead them to their twofold goal: the Supreme Pontiff to lead them to eternal life and the Emperor to lead them to temporal happiness. But to reach that harbor the human race must be freed from the alluring waves of greed so as to rest in the tranquillity of peace. This is the task to which the Emperor must devote his energies. His office is to provide freedom and peace for humans during their testing-time in this world.

The Monarch's authority derives directly from God, yet he is not excluded from all subordination to the Roman Pontiff, since in a certain way our temporal happiness is subordinate to our eternal happiness. The Emperor must observe that reverence toward Peter which a firstborn son owes to his father. When he is enlightened by the light of paternal grace he may the more enlighten the world, at the head of which he was placed by the One Who alone is ruler of all things spiritual and temporal. (*Monarchy* 3:16)

Reflection

The Second Vatican Council stressed everyone's responsibility to "renew the temporal order and make it increasingly more perfect: such is God's design for the world." The council asserted that "institutions of the political community, international relations, and so on . . . are not merely helps" to the final goal of the human race: "They possess a value of their own, placed in them by God. . . . Far from depriving the temporal order of its autonomy, of its specific ends, of its own laws and resources, or its importance for human well-being," God's design raises the temporal order "to the level of man's integral vocation here below" (*Decree on the Apostolate of Lay People* [*Apostolicam Actuositatem*, 1965], no. 7).

Dante in many outstanding ways anticipated the council's teaching on the value and autonomy of the temporal order. For him that teaching was one of two ultimate goals ordained by God. He energetically and tirelessly promoted peace and justice in this world in spite of much resistance and hostility. Besides his *Monarchy*, a frontal attack on papal temporal rule, he wrote numerous letters to Italian princes and cities, urging them to support the emperor, Henry VII, who was indeed a just and good ruler who could have brought about peace and justice, the conditions for human happiness in this world. But the greed and lust for power that obsessed the popes and princes kept Italy and Europe in war and misery for centuries.

✧ Review your civic responsibilities. Do you vote for candidates committed to social justice and peace, sincere defenders of human rights and human life?

✧ Your own neighborhood could be the place for many activities of peace and justice. Think of some concrete ways to be "a servant" to a neighbor or neighbors with some particular need. Then take action.

✧ Dante's vision of universal peace under one just ruler seems to us today utopian and unrealistic, yet it expresses a real, deep human desire—an echo within us of God's will. Reflect on Dante's famous words: "In His will is our peace. It is that sea to which all moves, both what He creates and what nature makes" (*Paradise* 3:85–87).

God's Word

They shall beat their swords into plowshares,
    and their spears into pruning hooks;
nation shall not lift up sword against nation,
    neither shall they learn war any more.

(Micah 4:3)

[God] has told you, O mortal, what is good;
    and what does the LORD require of you
but to do justice, and to love kindness,
    and to walk humbly with your God?

(Micah 6:8)

Closing prayer:

Glory to God in the highest heaven,
    and on earth peace among those whom he favors!

(Luke 2:14)

The Laity in the Church

Theme: The laity's prophetic office and "sense of the faith" are God's gifts for the common good of the church.

Opening prayer: God, you grant many and various gifts to all members of your church. Activate those gifts within us for the good of all the church.

About Dante

Dante the layman loved the church, his "most loving Mother and Bride of Christ," with a childlike tenderness and a zealous ferocity. He was deeply wounded and angered when her leaders defiled her by their greed, abuse of sacred powers, nepotism, heresy, and worldly ambition. He assigned several popes to hell for their sin of simony. Among them was Boniface VIII, whom Dante personally detested as the one responsible for his exile. Yet Dante was outraged when Boniface was assaulted by agents of the French king at Anagni. He described the attack on Christ's vicar as a re-crucifixion of Christ (see *Purgatory* 20:87). His reverence for the papal office never diminished.

When the French monarchy gained control over the Papacy with the election of a Frenchman, Pope Clement V, and the Papacy was transferred from Rome to Avignon in France, Dante was overcome with righteous indignation. Clement, a shameless nepotist and puppet of the French king, ruled from Avignon for ten years. Upon his death in 1314 the cardinals met near Avignon to elect a new pope. Almost all of them were French; only six were Italian. Dante wrote them a forceful letter exhorting them to reform themselves and the church and to bring the Papacy back to Rome. But the Italian cardinals were driven out of the conclave by the French, and after two years another Frenchman was elected, John XXII, one of the worst popes in history, condemned later by Pope Adrian VI as a heretic. In Paradise Dante had Saint Peter angrily denounce John XXII, Clement V, and Boniface VIII. Peter then commissions Dante to speak out on Earth against them (see *Paradise* 27:66).

In his letter to the Italian cardinals Dante compared himself to the prophet Jeremiah lamenting Jerusalem in ruins. Jeremiah had blamed the city's ruin on a corrupt priesthood. Dante likened the cardinals to the unruly oxen that dragged the ark of the Covenant into the wilderness. He targeted their intense study and manipulation of canon law to make themselves rich, and their neglect of the fathers of the church, who worshiped God, not gold. At the end he respectfully exhorted them to change and act courageously, not only for the good of the church but also for the "whole human community on pilgrimage here."

Pause: Does your love for the church move you to speak out courageously for reforms?

Dante's Words

Truly I am one of the least of the sheep in the pasture of Jesus Christ; truly I abuse no pastoral authority, since I possess no riches. By the grace, not of riches, but of God, "I am what I am" and the "zeal for His house has consumed me." For even from "the mouth of babes and sucklings" comes the truth pleasing to God. The man born blind confessed the truth which the Pharisees not only concealed but tried maliciously to pervert. These are the justification for my boldness. . . .

Among so many who usurp the office of shepherd, among so many sheep who, if not driven away, are neglected and left untended in the pastures, one voice alone, one alone of childlike loyalty, and that of a private individual, is heard at the funeral, as it were, of Mother Church.

And what wonder? Each one has taken greed as his wife, as you yourselves have done. Greed, the mother of malice and injustice! Ah! Most loving Mother, Spouse of Christ, by water and the Spirit you bear sons to your shame!

But, my Fathers, do not think I am unique in the world. Everyone is murmuring or thinking what I cry aloud. Some are simply stunned and amazed, but they do not testify to what they have seen. . . . Now I am forced to raise my voice: you have compelled me. You should be ashamed to receive rebuke and correction from so lowly a source. (*Epistle XI* 9–19)

Reflection

In this letter and in many passages of his works Dante courageously exercised the "prophetic office" of the laity, which the Second Vatican Council later proclaimed so clearly (see the *Dogmatic Constitution on the Church* [*Lumen Gentium*, 1964], no. 35). According to the council, the popes and bishops of Dante's time, in their contempt for the laity, did not recognize that

the laity are empowered—indeed sometimes obliged—to manifest their opinion on those things which pertain to the good of the Church. If the occasion should arise this should be done . . . with truth, courage and prudence and with reverence and charity towards those who, by reason of their office, represent the person of Christ. (No. 37)

The truths Dante proclaimed so boldly were eventually confirmed by popes and councils long after his lifetime. Dante's fierce denunciation of the secular power wielded by the popes of his time was finally vindicated in the nineteenth century when the popes were constrained to surrender their rule over the papal states. Many doctrines of faith clarified at Vatican Council II, such as the salvation of the nonbaptized, had already been taught by Dante (see *Paradise* 19–20). Centuries before John Cardinal Newman and Vatican Council II, Dante exercised his "sense of the faith," a spiritual gift shared by all the faithful; and even though not "consulted" by the hierarchy (they condemned his opinions!), he contributed greatly to the development of Catholic faith and spirituality.

Many popes from the Renaissance to our times have lavishly praised Dante. For the sixth centenary of Dante's death (1921) Pope Benedict XV issued an encyclical on Dante, the "pride and glory of humanity" (*On Dante*, no. 1). On the seventh centenary of Dante's birth (1965) Pope Paul VI extolled Dante's Catholic faith, his great love for Christ and the church, and his reverence for the vicar of Christ. He said, "Dante is the universe of nature and of grace in a single work of poetry" (Guitton, p. 119). "For a layman of the twentieth century," Paul VI remarked, "that layman's work is exemplary" (p. 128). Ironic kudos from the Vatican for Dante, whose *Monarchy* was among the first books placed on the Index of Forbidden Books for its condemnation of papal political power!

✧ Exercise your prophetic office and sense of the faithful by making a list of reforms that the church of the twenty-first century should undertake. Begin with reforms involving yourself and move on to reforms involving your parish, your diocese, and the universal church. Plan to take appropriate action—through your parish council and other proper channels—with truth, courage, prudence, reverence, and charity. According to Vatican Council II, the hierarchy "should with paternal love consider attentively in Christ initial moves, suggestions and desires proposed by the laity" (*Dogmatic Constitution on the Church*, no. 37).

✧ According to Dante the whole human community needs the light—the sun!—of the church's moral and spiritual leadership. Examine your conduct. Is it a light in a world whose culture sometimes glorifies self-gratification, greed, and contempt for human life?

✧ Reflect on the church as your mother, in whose baptismal womb you were reborn. Do you feel shame and sadness when her honor is disgraced by the immoral behavior of the clergy? Do you also consider your own misconduct—perhaps greed, indifference to the poor, and tolerance of evils such as abortion, war, and violation of human rights?

God's Word

Now there are varieties of gifts, but the same Spirit; and there are varieties of services, but the same Lord; and there are varieties of activities, but the same God who activates all of them in everyone. To each is given the manifestation of the Spirit for the common good. (Vv. 4–7)

Now you are the body of Christ and individually members of it. And God has appointed in the church first apostles, second prophets, third teachers. (1 Corinthians 12:27–28)

Closing prayer: God, give me courage to use my spiritual gifts with prudence and charity for the common good of your church.

✧ **Meditation 12** ✧

Endurance and Hope

Theme: Sufferings and disappointments in life oppress our soul, but hope in God's promises and unfailing love gives us the power of endurance.

Opening prayer: God, give us hope in your constant love and power when we are crushed by affliction, disappointment, and failure.

About Dante

Dante endured many hardships, losses, disappointments, and failures in his life: his parents' early deaths, Beatrice's death, the ruin of his political career and good reputation, the injustice of his exile, which deprived him of wife, children, and property. The poverty and homelessness of those nineteen years of banishment! And if that were not enough, he encountered everywhere in Italy bloody strife and warfare, perpetrated by greedy princes and church leaders. The church and the empire were devastated by avarice and lust for power. "The seamless garment of Christ (the unity of the church and the empire) was torn apart on the nail of greed" (*Monarchy* 1:16).

Dante described this pathetic condition of the church and the world in allegorical scenes in the Garden of Eden atop Purgatory. He saw the once glorious chariot (the church) suffering throughout its history a series of attacks and catastrophes—schisms, heresies, and acquisition of wealth and worldly power. The last scene depicts the church in Dante's time with images from the Book of Revelation: after being ripped apart by a dragon, the church becomes a hideous monster sprouting seven heads and ten horns. On it sits a whore (Pope Boniface VIII) kissing a jealous giant (the French king Philip the Fair). Their political alliances, greed, and power struggles are the culmination of centuries of corruption.

After Dante witnesses these horrific scenes, Beatrice prophesies that God will send someone to restore the church and empire. The identity of the future savior is purposely vague, but Beatrice commissions Dante to carry to Earth the message that God's justice and design have been violated by church leaders and kings. Her message is two edged: it addresses the urgent need for reform, and the hope of future salvation for the church and society. Dante becomes a prophet sent by God's Wisdom (Beatrice) to the world and church of his time.

Dante fearlessly proclaimed the message of divine judgment and hope, and endured much suffering for doing so. No doubt he suffered many temptations to despair—and perhaps even to suicide—but his hope in God, who could and would accomplish peace and justice, never failed.

Pause: The church and the world will always need radical reform. For you, is that a reason for despair, apathy, or hope-filled action?

Dante's Words

Beatrice said to me, "I want you from now on to free yourself from fear and shame. . . . Know that the vessel [the church] which the serpent broke was and is not. . . . The eagle [the empire] that shed feathers on the chariot that became a monster, then a prey, will not remain forever without heirs; I tell you this because I clearly see those stars, already near, that will bring us a time—its arrival nothing can hinder—in which a five-hundred, ten, and five shall be sent by God, to slay the giant and the thievish whore with whom he sins. . . .

"Repeat my words as you teach those who live that life which is merely a race to death. When you write, be sure that you describe the sad condition of the tree [God's justice] which you saw despoiled not once but twice on this spot. Whoever robs this tree or breaks its limbs sins against God. . . . The first soul who tasted of that tree longed in pain and desire more than five thousand years for Him Who paid the penalty Himself." (*Purgatory* 33:30–63)

Reflection

The mysterious prophecy that Dante expressed in numbers is probably a Kabbalistic code for the Latin word *dux* (leader) or for the Italian name of Henry VII, who was crowned emperor in 1310, but received more opposition than support and died suddenly in 1313. Dante had hoped that Henry, the just ruler sent by God, would restore peace and unity to the world. In a letter to Henry, Dante, like another John the Baptist, hailed the emperor as "the Lamb of God" as well as the second suffering servant of God, foretold by Isaiah. By bestowing such titles on Henry, Dante boldly asserted that the monarch too was a vicar of Christ on earth. "We believe and hope in you, proclaiming you to be the servant of God and son of the Church. You are all that the monarch should be: the height of loving-kindness and mercy" (*Epistle VII* 8). Dante believed that the monarch "can be the purest incarnation of justice, in which charity, rightly-ordered love, is most intense" (*Monarchy* 1:11).

Dante never doubted that the pope was the vicar of Christ in spiritual matters. The prelate's life should also be like Christ's: "The form of the Church is none other than the life of Christ, His deeds and words. His life was the model and example for the whole Church on earth, for its pastors in particular, but above all for the chief pastor whose mission is to feed the lambs and sheep" (3:15). The two "suns" appointed by God—the pope and the monarch—have complementary missions, and both have Christ as their model.

Sadly, most of the popes in Dante's time were the very antithesis of Christ. Dante even considered the papal seat vacant of a true vicar of Christ. This absence and the premature death of Henry caused him acute pain and disappointment, but he maintained his hope with patient endurance. In *The Comedy* Beatrice presents Dante to Saint James, the Apostle of hope, with the words: "There is no son of the Church Militant with greater hope than his. This is why he is allowed to come from Egypt to behold Jerusalem before his fighting days on earth are over" (*Paradise* 25:52–57).

✧ Disappointments and failures can cause frustration and even acute depression. Dante, who lost everything—family, property, career, and reputation—can serve for us as an example of endurance. Rather than wallow in self-pity, he transformed his exile into a time of stupendous creativity. He gave us *The Divine Comedy!* How might you transform your own times of "exile"?

✧ Pain and suffering can bring us to realize that we depend on God for the power and strength to move on in our lives with hope. Saint Paul, in the midst of "weaknesses, insults, hardships, persecutions, and calamities," could write, "Whenever I am weak, then I am strong" (2 Corinthians 12:10).

✧ Hope seems to have been Dante's strongest virtue. He often wrote of it, as in Purgatory when he meets Manfred, twice excommunicated, who repented while dying alone and was saved by God's mercy: "By the Church's curse no one is so lost that the Eternal Love cannot still return if hope reveals the slightest hint of green" (*Purgatory* 3:133–135). The church may fail us, all kinds of sufferings may afflict us, but communion with God can be kept alive by hope in God's love, which never fails us.

God's Word

Be patient, therefore, beloved, until the coming of the Lord. The farmer waits for the precious crop from the earth, being patient with it until it receives the early and the late rains. You also must be patient. Strengthen your hearts. . . . As an example of suffering and patience, beloved, take the prophets who spoke in the name of the Lord. Indeed we call blessed those who showed endurance. You have heard of the endurance of Job, and you

have seen the purpose of the Lord, how the Lord is compassionate and merciful. (James 5:7–11)

Closing prayer:

I cry to you out of the depths, O God. I wait for God and
place my hope in God's word. My soul waits for God
more than those who watch for the morning—yes, more
than those who watch for the morning. Place your hope
in God: with God there is steadfast love and great power
to save! (Adapted from Psalm 130:1–7)

✧ Meditation 13 ✧

Franciscan Spirituality

Theme: Franciscan spirituality, centered on Jesus' humanity, suffering, and loving service, radically renewed medieval Christians. It still compellingly calls us back to the essence of being a Christian.

Opening prayer: "Most high and glorious God, enlighten the darkness of my heart and give me right faith, certain hope, and perfect love and wisdom to do your holy will" (Saint Francis's prayer before the crucified Jesus; in Caroli, p. 143).

About Dante

Some Franciscan scholars claim that Dante was a Franciscan novice in Florence but left the order before taking vows. There is little reliable documentation for that claim. It is more likely that later in life he joined the Third Order of Saint Francis in Ravenna. There in his last few years he was close to the friars. He was buried in their church, perhaps dressed in the Franciscan habit. To this day the friars have guarded his remains against attempts to remove them to Florence.

By Dante's time the Franciscan movement had blossomed and spread—like a springtime of spiritual renewal—throughout Italy. The life of Francis and Franciscan spirituality had a powerful impact on Dante's soul, life, and works. Dante admired many saints, but considered Francis the one, after Mary, most like Jesus.

As a young man in Florence, Dante may have heard the great Franciscan theologian Saint Bonaventure, "the Seraphic Doctor," preach at Santa Croce. Among the teachers there was Friar Ubertino da Casale, author of *The Tree of the Crucified Life of Jesus,* a mystical work whose influence can be seen in Dante's *Comedy.* The many works of Bonaventure, especially his *Soul's Journey into God* and his *Life of Saint Francis,* made a deep impression on Dante's spirituality and his *Comedy.*

The artist Giotto, an intimate friend of Dante's and a kindred soul, painted a cycle of frescoes on the life of Saint Francis in the upper church of the Basilica of Saint Francis in Assisi. In the lower church another painting by Giotto shows Saint Francis helping three persons to ascend: a Franciscan friar, a poor Clare, and a Third Order member; the last is thought to be a portrait of Dante. The two friends and their artistic works were profoundly inspired by the new Franciscan spirit. Giotto's frescoes in Padua, painted while Dante was a guest in his home there, express dramatically the humanity and suffering of Jesus, the wellspring of Franciscan spirituality.

Pause: Do you nourish your soul on the classics of Christian spirituality, such as the works of Saint Bonaventure?

Dante's Words

In Paradise Dante had Saint Thomas Aquinas, a Dominican friar, give a stirring eulogy of Saint Francis. The following is an excerpt:

> While still a youth he opposed his father because he loved a lady to whom all would bar their door as if to death itself. Before the bishop and his father he took her for his wife, and from day to day he loved her more and more. She, bereft of her first husband for eleven hundred years and more, despised and ignored, remained without a lover until he came. . . . Francis and Lady Poverty are

the lovers in this story. Their sweet harmony and happy faces—their love, wonder, and tender looks—caused holy thoughts in others' hearts. . . . Later, urged by a thirst for martyrdom in the proud presence of the Sultan of Egypt, he preached Christ, but finding no one ripe for harvest there, returned to reap a crop in Italian fields. Then on the harsh rock between the Tiber and the Arno he received from Christ the final seal [the stigmata], which his body bore for two years. (*Paradise* 11:58–108)

Reflection

In the eulogy for Saint Francis, Dante had Thomas Aquinas introduce Francis as one of two "noble princes" (*Paradise* 11:35)—the other is Dominic—sent by Divine Providence to the church so that "the Bride of that Sweet Groom, who crying loud espoused her with His blood, might go to her Beloved made more secure within herself and also more faithful to her Spouse" (11:31–34). These two guides, sent by God's Wisdom, both had the same goal: to reform the church. Francis "shone with seraphic love"; Dominic "by his wisdom radiated cherubic splendor" (11:37–39).

Dante compared Francis's birth to the rising sun, "whose invigorating powers soon penetrated the earth with a new strength." Dante's brief biography of Francis focuses on the man's poverty, love, and likeness to Christ. Poverty for Dante was the antidote for greed, the deadly sin that had brought much misery and corruption to the church and society. Francis had embraced poverty as a wonderful liberator who opened his heart and life to love and serve all God's creatures.

Although forced into poverty by his exile, Dante nonetheless experienced its liberating power. After overcoming some bitterness and self-pity, he lived the Franciscan spirit as a layman dedicated to peace and service to the world. He wrote:

It is not only those who by their dress and form of life make themselves similar to Saint Benedict, Saint Augustine, Saint Francis, or Saint Dominic who devote themselves to a religious life; even those who are still in the married state can devote themselves to a life that is in the full and true sense religious, for what God wishes to be religious in us is simply our hearts. (*Banquet* 4,28:9)

✧ By living literally the words of the Gospel, Francis, a layman, renewed himself, the church, and the society of his time. Read and reflect on Jesus' Sermon on the Mount (Matthew, chapters 5–7). Let Jesus' words penetrate into your heart and renew your vision, values, and actions.

✧ In Bonaventure's *Life of Saint Francis (Legenda Maior)*, Jesus, from an image of the Crucifixion, tells Francis: "Go and repair my house. You see it is completely in ruins" (translated from Caroli, p. 525). Francis obeys by repairing the ruined little church of San Damiano in Assisi; then he realizes that the house Jesus refers to is Christ's universal church. Review your support of your local church—by money and personal service. Look at your contributions to the universal church. Many of the church's "living stones" are poor, hungry, and in need of your support.

✧ Contemplate photos or descriptions of Giotto's paintings of Jesus' life. Notice how Jesus' humanity, emotions, and sufferings are realistically portrayed—in a startling departure from the rigid Byzantine style of Giotto's time. The impact of Francis's spirituality on Giotto's art is striking. Giotto's icons can lead you to adore "God's humanity"—God's birth, life, and death for you.

God's Word

[Jesus said:] "If any want to be my followers, let them deny themselves and take up their cross and follow me. For those who want to save their life will lose it, and those who lose their life for my sake, and for the sake of the gospel, will save it. For what will it profit them to gain the whole world and forfeit their life?" (Mark 8:34–36)

Closing prayer: "God, grant that I may seek not so much to be loved as to love. For it is in giving of ourselves that we receive, and in dying that we are born to eternal life" (adapted from the Peace Prayer of Saint Francis).

Mary, Our Mother

Theme: Mary, humble and exalted, is our loving and powerful mother as well as our companion in faith.

Opening prayer: "Blessed are you among women, and blessed is the fruit of your womb" (Luke 1:42).

About Dante

In the Middle Ages devotion to Mary had reached such a degree of enthusiasm that her presence was everywhere—in the church's art, architecture, and liturgy; in university debates; and in the daily private prayers of the faithful. She was the air breathed by medieval Christians. Dante tells us, "I always invoke the name of that beautiful flower every morning and evening" (*Paradise* 33:89). It is no surprise that upon the death of Beatrice he would place her under Mary's protection: "The God of Justice called this most gracious one to glory under the banner of that blessed Queen, the Virgin Mary, whose name was always uttered with the greatest reverence by the blessed Beatrice" (*New Life* 28).

As a medieval Christian, Dante perceived instinctively (by the "sense of the faithful") that God's "maternal" love was mediated to him through Mary, the mother of Christ and his heavenly mother. In *The Comedy* Mary's compassionate love for Dante sets in motion the whole process of his conversion and salvation. She commissions Saint Lucy to send Beatrice down to Hell to enlist Virgil's help in saving Dante. Beatrice tells Virgil, "In heaven there is a gracious lady who grieves so much for what happened to the one I send you to, that her compassion breaks heaven's stern judgment" (*Inferno* 2:94–96).

As Virgil guides Dante up the seven stories of Purgatory, they see the souls purifying themselves of the seven deadly sins and learning the opposite virtues. On each level they learn by examples presented to them. The first example of each virtue is always Mary. On the first terrace—the purging of pride—they contemplate a carved image of the Annunciation. There Mary is humbly responding, "Behold the handmaid of God." By her submission to God's will "she turned the key, opening for us the Highest Love" (*Purgatory* 10:44).

In Paradise Dante enjoys three visions of Mary. In the first she is one of the saved in Christ's triumphant harvest, depicted as a beautiful garden under Christ, the sun. Beatrice calls Dante's attention to Mary, "the Rose in which God's Word took on flesh." Then Mary, together with all the blessed, follows her Son into the highest Heaven. The blessed, like children looking up to their nursing mother, lovingly and sweetly sing the *Regina Coeli*—"Queen of Heaven, rejoice!" (*Paradise* 23:121–129).

In the second vision Dante sees Mary enthroned in the highest seat of the Rose of Paradise. Just below her is Eve, "whose wound Mary closed and healed" (32:4). On the third tier is Beatrice, along with Rachel and other Hebrew women.

The third vision is a close-up of Mary's face. Saint Bernard, Dante's guide at this point, tells him, "Now look at that face which resembles Christ the most, for only in its radiance will you be able to look at Christ" (32:85). Bernard, glowing with childlike love for Mary, then praises her and begs her to grant Dante the final grace—the vision of God.

Pause: Do you relate to Mary as your heavenly mother who mediates God's compassionate, maternal love for you?

Dante's Words

Virgin Mother, daughter of your Son, humble and exalted more than any creature, chosen by God in His eternal plan! You are the one who so ennobled human nature that its Maker did not disdain to make Himself human. In your womb was rekindled the Love Whose warmth made this flower bloom in this eternal peace.

For all up here you are the noonday torch of charity, and below among mortals you are the living spring of hope. Lady, you are so great, so powerful, that those who seek grace without recourse to you would have their wish fly upward without wings. Your loving-kindness not only helps those who ask but often flows to them before their request.

In you is mercy, in you is pity, in you generosity; in you unites all that is good in God's creatures. This man, who from the lowest pit of the universe up to here has seen one by one the lives of souls, begs you that you grant him through your grace the power to raise his vision still higher toward the final blessedness. (*Paradise* 33:1–27)

Reflection

This prayer, spoken in *Paradise* by Saint Bernard, "the last of the Fathers," sums up over a thousand years of Marian devotion, expressed in the writings of the fathers and mothers of the church. In the third century Origen wrote that "to understand John's Gospel one must rest on Jesus' breast and receive from Him Mary as his mother also" (translated from Preuschen). This traditional devotion to Mary developed into the Middle Ages and received perhaps its strongest impulse and most tender expression from Bernard, Mary's greatest troubadour. His love for Mary inspired Dante to compose this magnificent prayer, which has been set to music by many composers, including Giuseppe Verdi.

Such praise of Mary may seem excessive, almost idolatrous, but the language of love is always extravagant. Bernard, Dante, and the other medieval Christians did not forget the fundamental truth that Mary also is one of the saved, redeemed by Christ. Beatrice, in the lowest sphere of Paradise, reminds Dante that the souls there are all in the one Paradise:

> "The seraphim who are nearest to God, Moses, Samuel, and the two Johns—and Mary too—all have their place in the same heaven. . . . Each one's bliss is equally eternal. All lend their beauty to the highest sphere, sharing one same sweet life to the degree that they feel the eternal breath of God." (*Paradise* 4:28–36)

Mary shares the same kind of glory as all other saints, but to a different degree. She is saved with all other creatures, but nonetheless she is the unique creature chosen and graced to be the mother of God's incarnate Son. Her uniqueness—exalted above all others—does not dissolve her solidarity with the rest of humanity. She, a daughter of Eve, is also the one destined by God to reverse humanity's fall by becoming the New Eve, the mother of a new humanity, saved and regenerated by her Son. Mary, humble and exalted, expresses the paradox of us all: our present journey of faith and our future glory. As a daughter of God and a humble woman of faith she is with us; as the mother of our God and Savior she is above us and for us—our advocate, queen, and mother, praying for our eternal glorification in Christ.

✧ A charming painting of the Madonna and Child was created by Pietro Lorenzetti, a contemporary of Dante's and a fellow Tuscan. It can be seen in the lower church of the Basilica of Saint Francis of Assisi. Mary and the child Jesus are flanked by Saint Francis and Saint John, the beloved disciple. Mary's thumb is pointing to Francis in answer to Jesus' question of who loves him more. Pray before your favorite icon of Mary and the child Jesus. Reflect on their love for you.

✧ In Saint Luke's description of the first Christian community in Jerusalem, "[Peter, John, James, and the other Apostles] were constantly devoting themselves to prayer, together with certain women, including Mary the mother of Jesus, as well as his brothers" (Acts of the Apostles 1:13–14). When you pray at the liturgy are you aware of the presence of Mary, the

Apostles, and other saintly women and men with you? Reflect on the mystery of the communion of saints, by which Mary and the other saints in heaven (along with all the pilgrims in purgatory and on earth) are also our companions and friends, praying with and for us.

✧ Carl Jung intuited that the human psychological need for a feminine, maternal God was filled in the person of Mary. By her divine maternity, Assumption, and coronation as queen of heaven, she entered into the Trinity and became a "divine" person. Jung rejoiced in the definition of the dogma of the Assumption in 1950 as a most important event for all Christians. Dante expressed the traditional belief in Mary's Assumption: in Paradise only Mary and Christ are clothed in the risen, glorified body (see *Paradise* 25:27). Reflect on Mary's Assumption as the sign and promise of your own final resurrection and "divinization."

✧ Read Gerard Manley Hopkins's poem "The Blessed Virgin Compared to the Air We Breathe." Among the beautiful verses are these:

> I say that we are wound
> With mercy round and round
> As if with air: the same
> Is Mary, more by name.
> She, wild web, wondrous robe,
> Mantles the guilty globe,
> Since God has let dispense
> Her prayers his providence.

(P. 159)

God's Word

And Mary said,
    "My soul magnifies the Lord,
        and my spirit rejoices in God my Savior,
    for he has looked with favor on the lowliness of his
        servant.
    Surely, from now on all generations will call me
        blessed;
    for the Mighty One has done great things for me."
                                  (Luke 1:46–49)

Closing prayer: Holy Mary, mother of God, pray for us sinners now and at the hour of our death.

✧ Meditation 15 ✧

Jesus, God's Incarnate Love

Theme: God's love became flesh and blood in the Son, who suffered and died on the cross for us.

Opening prayer: O God, may your love, poured out in the Incarnation and Crucifixion of your Son, flood and inebriate my heart.

About Dante

Dante loved theology. At the Franciscan and Dominican schools in Florence, he attended the lectures of friars who had studied theology under Thomas Aquinas and Bonaventure in Paris. Later he too studied theology in Paris. During his exile he stayed at Benedictine monasteries whose great libraries gave him access to the Bible, the works of the Fathers, and the summas of the medieval Scholastics. All those sources deeply influenced Dante's works.

Theology in the Middle Ages was the province of the clergy and the religious. Yet Dante the layman was acclaimed a great theologian immediately after his death. At his funeral the eulogist, Guido da Polenta, called on Italian poets to compose a poem for Dante's epitaph. From among the many responses Boccaccio judged the best to be that of Giovanni del Virgilio, a longtime friend of Dante's. It began with the Latin words *Theologus Dantes* (Dante the theologian), then praised him as an inspired poet who "returned to the stars" (see Dinsmore, pp. 94–95). Boccaccio too praised Dante as a supreme theologian and great poet. In Boccaccio's view "theology and poetry are, as it were, one, for their subject is the same. Theology is a poetry about God" (translated from Boccaccio, *Trattatello in Laude di Dante*).

In 1373 Boccaccio gave the first public lectures on *The Comedy* in Dante's parish church in Florence. Even earlier (in 1327) a Franciscan theologian had lectured on Dante's *Comedy* to his fellow friars in their great Florentine church, Santa Croce. But in 1335 the Dominicans had solemnly condemned Dante's works as heretical and forbidden their friars to read them. The papal curia in Avignon wanted the works burned publicly.

In 1414 a Franciscan theologian and bishop, Giovanni da Serravalle, translated *The Comedy* into Latin for his fellow bishops from all over Europe. In his preface he noted that a theologian's knowledge about God is not enough: it should penetrate into the theologian's heart and become ardent love for God. He described Dante as a theologian who both knew and loved God. Dante's teacher, Beatrice, theology personified, had led Dante into the beatific love of God. A Franciscan would recognize in Dante the ardor of Saint Francis, who inspired Bonaventure and through him Dante. Serravalle derived Dante's name in Latin, *Dantes*, from the Latin *dans* (one who gives) and the Greek *theos* (God). Dante, he claimed, gives us God in poetry.

Pause: Have you noticed that theology is best expressed in poetry: the prophets' words, the Psalms, Jesus' words, the church's hymns?

Dante's Words

Among the many theology lessons Beatrice gives her student Dante in Paradise, the one in canto 7 stands out as a miniature summa—a summary of Christian faith encompassing the Creation, Fall, Redemption, and Final Resurrection. Its Christ-centered focus is the Incarnation and Crucifixion—the greatest act of God's love. It explains: "The human race lay sick below within its sin for long centuries until God's Word chose to descend. There, moved by His unselfish love alone, He took unto Himself in His own person that nature which had wandered from its Maker." When Dante asks why God chose to redeem us by means of Christ's death on the cross, Beatrice responds:

> The reason, brother, for that choice is buried from the eyes of everyone whose understanding is not matured within love's flame. . . . Since the deed gratifies more the doer, the more it manifests the goodness of the heart from which it springs, the Divine Goodness, Who puts His imprint on the world, was pleased to use all His means to raise you up again. Between the last night and the first day there has never been nor will there be so exalted and so magnificent an act! For God was more bounteous by giving Himself in raising you up than if He had simply remitted your debt. (*Paradise* 7:28–117)

Reflection

These few words reveal our poet as a theologian whose understanding was "matured within love's flame." Dante's sacred poem from beginning to end is a heartfelt song to God's love. In the beginning he looks up from his dark forest and sees "the sun rising with the other stars, which were with it on the world's first day when Divine Love set them in motion" (*Inferno* 1:37–40). At the end his heart is moved by "the Love Who moves the sun and the other stars" (*Paradise* 33:145).

For Dante, God's love, which created the universe, reached its climax in the Incarnation and Crucifixion of God's Son. Dante chose Good Friday of 1300 as the starting point of his vision and journey. It was also 25 March, the feast of the Incarnation (the Annunciation), which in the Florentine calendar was the first day of the new year. The coincidence of the Incarnation and Crucifixion—the most magnificent act of God's love—is the heart of Dante's theology and spirituality, as it is still for us today.

Dante's three visions of Christ in Paradise focus on the cross and the Incarnation. In the first vision, Christ shines on the cross together with the martyrs, sparkling lights moving on it. The sight so moves Dante's heart that he offers himself to Christ as a holocaust (*Paradise* 14). In the second vision, Christ as the sun shines on his beloved garden—all the blessed— where Mary is the rose in which God's love became incarnate. Christ leads Mary and the blessed up with him in a triumphant ascension (23). In the final vision, Christ is the central circle of the Trinity. Dante cannot comprehend how "our image" is there in the circle. The mystery of the Incarnation baffles his mind, but a flash of understanding reveals it. Dante's poetic skill fails him, but he says, "Like a wheel in perfect balance turning, I felt my will and desire impelled by the Love Who moves the sun and the other stars"—the final words of *The Comedy*.

Dante's vision faded, but, he said, "the sweetness left by it I can still feel distilling in my heart" (*Paradise* 33:63). He prayed to God that he might capture just one spark of God's glorious love revealed to him so that he could leave it for future generations in his verses. I believe his prayer was answered. His *Comedy* is his gift from God to us. Dante's Franciscan translator wisely interpreted his name as meaning "one who gives God." Dante has given us a spark of God's love, which still ignites our hearts.

✧ When Saint John in Paradise asks Dante "how many teeth had bitten his heart into loving God," Dante gives a long list, in the middle of which is "the death He died so that I may live" (*Paradise* 26:58–66). Make a mental or written list of God's many acts of love for you that move your heart to love God.

✧ The two most common scenes depicted on the walls and altarpieces in the medieval churches of Italy are the Annunciation and the Crucifixion, both of which usually portray the Trinity. In the Annunciation the Father sends the Spirit as a dove on Mary, who conceives Jesus. In the Crucifixion the Father offers us the Son on the cross as the Spirit hovers above and Mary and John stand below. Such icons invite the beholder to enter into the mystery of God's love. Contemplate an icon of the Annunciation or the Crucifixion and let yourself be drawn into the circle of God's love.

✧ The Incarnation and Crucifixion are marvelously present in the Eucharist. Among the many eucharistic hymns composed around Dante's time is the *Ave, Verum Corpus*, still sung today to Mozart's sublime music. This translation may move your heart to prayer:

> Hail, true Body, born of the Virgin Mary, which truly suffered and was offered on the cross for us; whose pierced side truly flowed with Blood! Be to us a foretaste of heaven when we are in the agony of death, O merciful, loving, sweet Jesus, Son of Mary. (Translated from Britt, p. 181)

God's Word

God's love was revealed among us in this way: God sent his only Son into the world so that we might live through him. In this is love, not that we loved God but that he loved us and sent his Son to be the atoning sacrifice for our sins. (1 John 4:9–10)

Closing prayer: "Holy Mother, make my heart glow and melt with love for your Son, my crucified God; make it inebriated with his blood and pierced by his wounds" (adapted from "Stabat Mater," a hymn composed by Jacopone da Todi, Franciscan friar, contemporary of Dante's; in Britt, p. 277).

B·E·A·U·T·Y

✧ Works Cited ✧

Augustine. *Confessions.* Trans. Henry Chadwick. New York: Oxford University Press, 1991.

Benedict XV, Pope. *On Dante.* In *The Papal Encyclicals, 1903–1939,* by Claudia Carlen Ihm.

Boccaccio, Giovanni. *Trattatello in Laude di Dante.* Ed. Pier Giorgio Ricci. Milan and Naples, 1965.

———. *Vita di Dante.* In *Aids to the Study of Dante,* Dinsmore.

Bosco, Umberto, gen. ed. *Enciclopedia Dantesca.* Vol. 6. Rome: Instituto della Enciclopedia Dantesca, Fondata da Giovanni Treccani, 1984.

Britt, Dom Matthew, ed. *The Hymns of the Breviary and Missal.* New York: Benziger Brothers, 1948.

Bruni, Leonardo. *Life of Dante.* In *Aids to the Study of Dante,* Dinsmore.

Caroli, Ernesto, gen. ed. *Fonti Francescane.* Assisi, Italy: Editrici Francescane, 1986.

Chesterton, Gilbert K. *Orthodoxy.* New York: Doubleday, Image Books, 1990.

Dinsmore, Charles Allen. *Aids to the Study of Dante.* Boston: Houghton Mifflin Company; Cambridge: Riverside Press, 1908.

Flannery, Austin, ed. *Vatican Council II: The Conciliar and Post Conciliar Documents.* 1988 rev. ed. Northport, NY: Costello Publishing Company, 1987.

Guitton, Jean. *The Pope Speaks: Dialogues of Paul VI with Jean Guitton.* Trans. Anne Fremantle and Christopher Fremantle. New York: Meredith Press, 1968.

Hopkins, Gerard Manley. *Gerard Manley Hopkins.* Ed. Catherine Phillips. Oxford: Oxford University Press, 1986.

International Commission on English in the Liturgy, English trans. *The Sacramentary.* New York: Catholic Book Publishing Company, 1985.

Preuschen, E., ed. *Der Johanneskommentar Origenes Werke* (The Commentary of Origen on Saint John's Gospel). Vol. 10, Die Griechischen Christlichen Schriftsteller. Leipzig, 1903.

Shakespeare, William. *Hamlet.* In *The London Shakespeare*, ed. John Munro, vol. 5, *The Tragedies.* New York: Simon and Schuster, 1957.

Vossler, Karl. *Mediaeval Culture: An Introduction to Dante and His Times.* Vol. 1. Trans. William Cranston Lawton. New York: Harcourt, Brace and Company, 1929.

✧ For Further Reading ✧

English Translations of Dante's Works

Alighieri, Dante. *The Banquet.* Trans. Christopher Ryan. Stanford French and Italian Studies. Saratoga, CA: Anma Libri and Company, 1989.

———. *De Vulgari Eloquentia.* English. Ed. and trans. Steven Botterill. Cambridge: Cambridge University Press, 1996.

———. *The Divine Comedy.* 3 vols. Trans. John Ciardi. New York: New American Library, Mentor. 1989.

———. *The Divine Comedy.* 3 vols. Trans. Mark Musa. New York: Penguin Books, 1984.

———. *The Divine Comedy.* 6 vols. Trans. Charles Singleton. Princeton, NJ: Princeton University Press, 1982.

———. *The Letter to Can Grande.* In *The Letters of Dante.* 2d ed. Trans. Paget Toynbee. Oxford: Clarendon Press, 1966.

———. *Monarchy, and Three Political Letters.* Trans. Donald Nicholl. London: Weidenfeld and Nicolson, 1954.

———. *The New Life.* In *Portable Dante,* Musa.

Musa, Mark, ed. and trans. *The Portable Dante.* New York: Penguin Books, 1995.

Books About Dante's Life and Works

Anderson, William. *Dante the Maker.* New York: Routledge, 1982.

Bergin, Thomas G., ed. *From Time to Eternity: Essays on Dante's "Divine Comedy."* New Haven: Yale University Press, 1967.

Berrigan, Daniel. *The Discipline of the Mountain: Dante's "Purgatorio" in a Nuclear World.* New York: Seabury Press, 1979.

Collins, James J. *Dante: Layman, Prophet, Mystic.* Staten Island, NY: Alba House, 1989.

———. *Pilgrim in Love: An Introduction to Dante and His Spirituality.* Chicago: Loyola University Press, 1984.

Freccero, John, ed. *Dante: A Collection of Critical Essays.* Englewood Cliffs, NJ: Prentice-Hall, 1965.

Gallagher, Joseph. *A Modern Reader's Guide to Dante's "The Divine Comedy."* Liguori, MO: Liguori Publications, 1999.

Hollander, Robert. *Allegory in Dante's "Commedia."* Princeton, NJ: Princeton University Press, 1969.

Jacoff, Rachel, ed. *The Cambridge Companion to Dante.* Cambridge: Cambridge University Press, 1993.

Jones, Alan W. *The Soul's Journey: Exploring the Three Passages of the Spiritual Life with Dante as a Guide.* [San Francisco]: HarperSanFrancisco, 1995.

Luke, Helen. *From Dark Wood to White Rose.* Pecos, NM: Dove Publications, 1975.

Mazzotta, Giuseppe. *Dante, Poet of the Desert: History and Allegory in "The Divine Comedy."* Princeton, NJ: Princeton University Press, 1979.

Sayers, Dorothy Leigh. *Further Papers on Dante.* London: Methuen, 1957.

———. *Introductory Papers on Dante.* London: Methuen, 1954.

Vossler, Karl. *Mediaeval Culture: An Introduction to Dante and His Times.* 2 vols. New York: Frederick Ungar Publishers, 1958.

Acknowledgments *(continued)*

The scriptural quotations contained herein are from the New Revised Standard Version of the Bible. Copyright © 1989 by the Division of Christian Education of the National Council of the Churches of Christ in the United States of America. All rights reserved.

The scriptural material described as adapted is freely paraphrased and is not to be used or understood as an official translation of the Bible.

The central memory of faith on page 57 and Memorial Proclamation of Faith II on page 58 are quoted from *The Sacramentary*, English translation prepared by the International Commission on English in the Liturgy (New York: Catholic Book Publishing Company, 1985), page 545. Illustrations and arrangement copyright © 1974 by Catholic Book Publishing Company, New York.

The words of the *Decree on the Apostolate of Lay People (Apostolicam Actuositatem,* 1965) on page 81 and of the *Dogmatic Constitution on the Church (Lumen Gentium,* 1964) on pages 85 and 86 are quoted from *Vatican Council II: The Conciliar and Post Conciliar Documents,* 1988 revised edition, edited by Austin Flannery, OP (Northport, NY: Costello Publishing Company, 1987), numbers 7 and 37. Copyright © 1975, by Harry J. Costello and Reverend Austin Flannery, OP.

Titles in the Companions for the Journey Series

Praying with Anthony of Padua *Praying with Ignatius of Loyola*

Praying with Benedict *Praying with John Baptist de La Salle*

Praying with C. S. Lewis *Praying with John Cardinal Newman*

Praying with Catherine McAuley *Praying with John of the Cross*

Praying with Catherine of Siena *Praying with Julian of Norwich*

Praying with the Celtic Saints *Praying with Louise de Marillac*

Praying with Clare of Assisi *Praying with Martin Luther*

Praying with Dante *Praying with Meister Eckhart*

Praying with Dominic *Praying with Mother Teresa*

Praying with Dorothy Day *Praying with Pope John XXIII*

Praying with Elizabeth Seton *Praying with Teresa of Ávila*

Praying with Francis of Assisi *Praying with Thérèse of Lisieux*

Praying with Francis de Sales *Praying with Thomas Aquinas*

Praying with Frédéric Ozanam *Praying with Thomas Merton*

Praying with Hildegard of Bingen *Praying with Vincent de Paul*

Order from your local religious bookstore or from

Saint Mary's Press
702 TERRACE HEIGHTS
WINONA MN 55987-1320
USA
800-533-8095
www.smp.org